# A Fishing Life
# is Hard Work

# A Fishing Life
# is Hard Work

Art Scheck

STACKPOLE
BOOKS

Copyright © 2003 by Stackpole Books

Published by
STACKPOLE BOOKS
5067 Ritter Road
Mechanicsburg, PA 17055
www.stackpolebooks.com

Printed in the United States

10  9  8  7  6  5  4  3  2  1

First Edition

**Library of Congress Cataloging-in-Publication Data**
Scheck, Art.
  A fishing life is hard work / Art Scheck.— 1st ed.
    p. cm.
  ISBN 0-8117-0041-0 (hardcover)
  1. Fly fishing—Anecdotes.  I. Title.

    SH456 .S29 2003

    799.1'24—dc21

                                                              200215

    2899

FOR MARY JO

# CONTENTS

# PREFACE

*Tom said to himself that it was not such a hollow world, after all. He had discovered a great law of human action, without knowing it—namely, that in order to make a man or a boy covet a thing, it is only necessary to make the thing difficult to attain. If he had been a great and wise philosopher, like the writer of this book, he would now have comprehended that Work consists of whatever a body is obliged to do, and that Play consists of whatever a body is not obliged to do. And this would help him to understand why constructing artificial flowers or performing on a treadmill is work, while rolling ten-pins or climbing Mont Blanc is only amusement. There are wealthy gentlemen in England who drive four-horse passenger-coaches twenty or thirty miles on a daily line, in the summer, because the privilege costs them considerable money; but if they were offered wages for the service, that would turn it into work and then they would resign.*

—Mark Twain, *Tom Sawyer*

When you get right down to it, Mark Twain selected and arranged words for a living. So do I, though not as well as Twain. It's like the difference between, say, designing the Cathedral of Notre

Dame and laying bricks, or between composing a symphony and playing drums for a three-chord punk-rock song. Some guys write *The Innocents Abroad* and *Huckleberry Finn;* others edit and write for fly-fishing magazines.

That my words have to do with fishing is a lucky break for me. There are, after all, publications with such titles as *Modern Proctologist* or *Industrial Adhesives Quarterly,* and someone has to get up every morning and edit them. Such jobs explain, in part, why stock in a liquor company is generally a good investment.

Still, work is work, and fishing, or at least editing and writing fishy stuff, has been my business for more than a decade. Half a dozen magazines, hundreds of articles, a bunch of books, a catalog or two, a house organ—as an editor or writer, I've inflicted millions of words on the angling public. I am obliged, every day, to think about fishing, talk with fisherfolk, deal with tackle-company and fishing-lodge publicists, study photos of fish or anglers or flies, and look for new developments in fly fishing, all while racing at least one deadline. I'm not complaining, mind you: God knows there are worse fates for a guy who likes to monkey around with words and punctuation.

While this racket has its moments and privileges, it's not all beer and skittles. I once asked a friend, an uncommonly prolific angling writer, how he manages to produce dozens—sometimes many dozens—of articles and at least one book a year.

"Fear," he said. "I write out of fear. The bills will keep coming whether or not I write. If I don't sell six articles a month, somebody will show up to turn off the electricity and another guy will come to repossess the car. My wife will have to call a cab to leave me."

That's work, no matter how you look at it, and it's the nature of the business for pretty nearly anyone who dives into it full-time. As in any job, having to meet a quota—sixty articles a year, six issues of a magazine, eight new fishing books for a spring catalog, thirty pages of advertising an issue—can do things to the product and the person who makes it, few of them good. This explains some of the drivel in magazines.

And a long immersion in the business of fishing can do things to a fisherman. Some guys burn out and turn their backs on both the business and the sport. Others become cynical hacks or shills for manufacturers. A few become drunkards. A relatively small number find a happy balance, a way to keep the lights on, keep their integrity, keep their perspective, and keep doing the best work they can. I've been lucky enough to work with some of these people, though I've also dealt with my share of the other kinds.

Maintaining my perspective, finding and keeping a balance between fishing as work and as play (and sometimes as much more than amusement), has been tricky for me, and I haven't always succeeded. Of course, the fulcrum of life's balance changes over time. I grew up fishing, and I haven't always found it easy to reconcile what I now do for money with something I've always done for me. Twelve years in the outdoor-ink game and the fishing business have colored my view of angling writers, fly-fishing purists, experts, hot new tackle, exotic destinations, and the publishing trade. Experience has scraped the rosy tint from my glasses and replaced it with a hue that provides clearer vision, at least for me.

Yet fishing itself, its reasons and rewards, doesn't change. I'm pretty sure that I've learned to enjoy it now for same reasons I enjoyed it thirty years ago. Maybe I'm a case of arrested development. Or maybe I'm just lucky.

The big decision in life is whether to laugh, cry, or get mad. I'd rather laugh. It helps make the whole affair a bit more like play than work. And it explains most of the pieces in this book.

*Anderson, South Carolina*
*April 2002*

## CHAPTER 1

# *Life in the Fast Water*

AN EDITOR OF GREAT WISDOM AND EXPERIENCE, MY FIRST AND BEST mentor in the fishing-magazine game, told a parable that didn't sink in for several years after I'd heard it.

Many years ago, Bob, the editor, went into New York on business. He made a couple of extra stops to visit friends in the trade and, coming out of an office building, bumped into a freelance photographer he hadn't seen in a while. Such things happen, even in Manhattan. They exchanged pleasantries, and Bob asked the photographer how business was.

"Great," the photographer said. "Just last week I landed a staff job with *Wanton*." The title belonged to a glossy magazine of the variety called "men's sophisticates" by newsstand distributors. At the time, many of them were still sold in plain brown wrappers and kept behind the drugstore counter.

Bob expressed joy and envy, and asked for details.

It was a fantastic gig, the photographer explained. He was going to get paid, and pretty well, for taking pictures of curvaceous and uninhibited lovelies as they shed the few, flimsy garments with which they began each shoot. The only problem, he joked, would be figuring out how to avoid steaming up the viewfinder.

It sounded like a problem worth solving, Bob joked back. He congratulated the photographer on his good fortune. A steady job with a pleasant subject doesn't come along every day. They chatted for another few minutes and parted.

They met again six months later, at a publishing-business party at the home of a mutual friend. Bob steered the photographer into a quiet corner.

"How's it going at *Wanton?*" he asked. "Gimme the details, bub. Omit nothing. And where are my free copies?"

"I'm not there anymore," the photographer said. "I quit. I had to. My wife was going to leave me."

Bob voiced condolences and began a philippic on women. Let a chemist analyze the female, he noted, and he'd come up with 97 percent jealousy. Can't *any* of them understand business?

"No, that's not it at all," the photographer said. "Cindy wasn't jealous. But after staring at naked chicks four days a week for four months, I kind of lost interest in sex. That's why my wife made me quit. Dereliction of duty, I guess."

Things were better now, the photographer said. Bob said he was glad to hear it. They returned to the party.

The wise old editor swore it was a true story. I didn't believe him at first. But later I did.

The fun didn't go out of fly fishing all at once. Angling had shaped my life since toddlerhood, and something you've loved for thirty-odd years doesn't become a drag overnight. But it didn't take very long, either. Within three years after starting my first job at an angling magazine, I'd stopped fishing. For the next twenty months, my rods and reels and waders sat in the back of a utility closet, behind toolboxes and lumber. Spiders built webs between the rod tubes; a thick layer of dust settled on boxes full of reels, fly boxes, spare lines, and leader spools. I tied flies and took photos of them to make magazine articles, then threw the flies in the trash. When I drove across a bridge, I no longer glanced down to check the water.

Burnout? Overexposure? Maybe. For a long time, I was putting in sixty to eighty hours a week editing, writing, and proofreading fishy stuff. That's how small-time publishing works. When you think and write about fly fishing every day for several years, always under deadline pressure and never sure if your job will still be there tomorrow, you might lose interest in actually going fishing. It's risky to make your passion your work, particularly when it turns out to be a risky business.

I had, in a sense, turned pro, and that changed both the causes and effects of fishing. Now that I had magazines to fill, I sometimes felt that I *should* go fishing—to find something to write about, to try a new fly pattern, to master a technique described in an article, to expand the expertise an editor is supposed to possess—and that feeling took the fun out of the game. Mark Twain was right when he explained the difference between work and play.

Mostly, though, I made the mistake of letting the tawdry side of the angling game pollute the sport. Like most people in it, I came into the fishing-magazine business by accident, and I came in believing the stuff I'd been reading. My first several years in the media racket were one long, tiring lesson in disenchantment. I wasn't ready for famous angling authors who can't string six words together without making seven mistakes, for advertisers who want "editorial support" in exchange for buying space, for publishers eager to print anything that helps sell an ad, for companies willing to swap free equipment or trips for glowing writeups, for writers and editors who cheerfully make the swap. Reading fishing magazines hadn't prepared me for life in the belly of the beast: the endless, desperate selling, colossal egos inflated by trivial accomplishments, the cynical recycling of clichés and idiocies, the fakes and liars, the general cheapness and ineptitude that so often seemed to define the entire business.

On my first day in the publishing trade, the senior editor to whom I answered summed up almost forty years of experience: "What we do here," he told me, "is a particularly cheap form of semi-journalism." Within a couple of years, I concluded that he was an optimist.

Of course I was naive. What reason had I to assume that publishing fishing magazines would be any more noble a business than, say, selling worn-out cars to poor folk? By the time I turned thirty, a bizarre assortment of jobs had taught me the universal ethic: do or say whatever will make the dollar move from the other guy's pocket to yours. Why should printing fish stories be any cleaner?

No reason at all. But it took me a while to learn that. Until I did, the business of angling nearly wrecked fishing for me. Disenchantment oozed from my job into trout streams and bass ponds, fouling things and places I'd loved. For a while, I thought of myself as an ex-fisherman. And my life had a big hole in it.

Oddly enough, I started to recover at a fishing-business affair. A big advertiser had invited a bunch of editors and writers, including me, to a media event at a swank saltwater destination. The company was to unveil a group of rods that would, like all new rods, change fly fishing as we knew it. We lucky members of the sporting press would enjoy free lodging and whiskey for two nights and receive examples of the new miracle sticks, on the safe assumption that we'd come home to craft encomiums that would drive hordes of readers to tackle shops.

Not to go would have been impolite and impolitic. Our competitors would be there. Although I hadn't thrown a fly in more than a year and a half, and really had no inclination to, I figured I'd take the free goodies graciously, make appropriate *ooohing* and *aahhing* sounds, suck up some of the host's Scotch, and beat it as early as good manners permitted. They'd get their write-up and we'd keep the advertising business. It's how the game works.

The invitation hinted at doing some striped-bass fishing. On the chance that I couldn't decently avoid it, I threw a pair of waders in the back of my truck, along with my duffel bag. I pointed the truck's rusty nose at a high-rent district on the New England coast and reconciled myself to a few days of acting.

Our hosts put us up in a lovely inn with a good bar and made it clear that we should not for a moment go thirsty. I knew more than half of the dozen or so writers and editors who had come, and the first afternoon and evening passed pleasantly enough.

The hype started after breakfast the next morning. We squeezed into a conference room and endured talks by engineers, marketing guys, and the company's press-relations man, then a videotape about how the new rods represented humanity's greatest technical breakthrough since Pythagoras figured out that deal with triangles, and then another speech and a couple of testimonials. It boiled down to the usual claptrap: lighter yet more powerful so that you can cast farther with less effort to catch more and bigger fish.

Then we got our free stuff. No one could fault our host's generosity. We each received a shiny new saltwater fly rod, a reel with line and backing, leaders, a complete fluorocarbon leader-making kit, a box of flies, a shirt emblazoned with the new rod's logo, and a cap ditto. Everything but the rod was packed in a fancy stripping basket. The rod came in a snazzy case with the recipient's name engraved on a brass plate. It remains the best one-day haul I've ever made.

After lunch, we toddled down to the beach to test-cast our new rods. Predictably, several editors worked up a sweat showing off their prowess. I found, to my relief, that I hadn't entirely forgotten how to cast; indeed, I remembered just well enough to tell that I didn't much like my new, expensive, high-performance rod. It had the action of a pool cue and a strange, dead feel, as if you were working it by remote control. Weeks later, a friend described casting with it as the fly-fishing equivalent of using a condom: you'll get the job done, but you won't feel much.

Naturally, we sporting journalists praised the new rods and lauded the singular genius of the men who had made them. Free whiskey and advertising contracts were at stake.

The test drives concluded, we listened to harangues by a couple of technical types who tried to prove, scientifically, that using the new rods must inevitably result in longer casts made with less effort and, it hardly needs saying, the capture of more and larger fish. We nodded and studied our press packages. A few guys took notes, or at least pretended to. Some, no doubt, joined me in wondering when the bar opened.

The evening's agenda called for striped-bass fishing. Guides and boats had been hired by our free-spending hosts. There seemed no way to avoid it—leaving would have given competitors something to talk about—so I joined several acquaintances on the inn's porch to get ready, a process that included taking steps to avoid dehydration.

Old habits die hard, and without giving the matter any thought, I started monkeying around with my leader. My new outfit had a one-piece leader attached to the floating fly line with a badly tied nail knot. I never like to trust someone else's rigging, and I prefer loop-to-loop connections. Without knowing why I was bothering, I cut the leader off, doubled about an inch of the line to make a small loop, and secured the loop with a pair of back-to-back nail knots tied with 10-pound-test material from my new leader kit. I tied a perfection loop in the butt of the leader and joined it to the line. Momentum took over, and a minute later I'd cut about four feet off the skinny end of the leader and tied a small surgeon's loop in what was left. Then I made up three loop-to-loop tippets with Bimini twists, one to go on the truncated leader and two to carry as spares. It's how I rig nearly all leaders, fresh or salt, a strong, simple system that lets me replace tippets without having to tie any knots on the water.

In for a penny, in for a pound. Between drinks, I stripped the entire line off the reel to check its connection to the backing and found another sloppy knot. I made a nail-knot loop on the tail end of the line, tied a long Bimini in the backing, and joined backing to line with a loop-to-loop junction. My chums on the porch seemed impressed by my preparations.

After a quick sandwich, three of us angling journalists and one of our hosts squeezed into a guide's SUV with a boat hitched to it and went in search of fish. We cast fruitlessly for half an hour at a beach next to a narrow inlet, flogged another beach for another thirty minutes with the same results, and then piled into the little boat to go try a big salt pond where, the guide assured us, the tide would be better. We'd beach the boat, he said, and then get out and wade.

Fly casting uses muscles in a unique way, and my out-of-shape arm was already tired from swinging the big, stiff rod. I'd been casting poorly, mostly from being out of practice, but partly because I'd been throwing a huge, overweight Clouser Minnow my companions and the local experts had recommended. I wasn't looking forward to another couple hours of work. But I was stuck.

We had a pleasant boat ride on an exceptionally beautiful evening, even by the standards of New England in late May. I tilted my head back and let the boat's speed force the saltwater scents into my nose.

Ten minutes later, our guide killed the big outboard, and the boat crunched onto a beach. Clumsy in our chest waders, we climbed over the gunwales and into the water. The guide indicated the direction of the current and suggested where we should spread out to fish. I offered to take the farthest spot.

It was about a two hundred-yard walk, much of it through waist-deep water. I moved slowly, as I always do when I wade anything bigger than a brook-trout stream, and felt the slightly creepy, vulnerable sensation I always get in strange water higher than my knees. A couple of crabs and small fish scurried away. A dense school of tiny baitfish changed direction to avoid me. By the time I reached my spot, most of my companions were already casting.

I fought with the strange, stiff rod and grotesquely heavy fly for about twenty minutes, slapping the water with my backcasts and throwing tailing loops and wishing the evening were over. My arm felt the way it did after raking a foot of snow off the roof. My left foot felt like that side of my waders had developed a leak. A hundred yards away, a couple of the guys kept up the kind of inane fishing chatter that some anglers find necessary.

After a spectacularly bad cast, I stripped in my line and looked at the big, heavy fly while I contemplated the situation. I was fishing in a place and with people not of my choosing, using tackle I didn't like and a fly I hadn't tied, sick to death of empty fishing babble and product hype and all the pretentious twaddle in which the sport and business are awash, going through the motions because it was my job, because one has to keep big advertisers happy by accepting their freebies and writing reviews, because one has to belong to the club to do business. For about thirty seconds, I hated fly fishing.

Then the utter ridiculousness of the scene and my attitude hit me as hard as my backcasts had been slapping the ocean. I was standing in clear water in a beautiful place on a lovely evening, with almost a thousand dollars' worth of new tackle in my hands, with nothing to do for the next hour but try to catch a fish, and I wasn't even close to having any fun. *That,* it dawned on me, was absurd.

Something had to give, and it did. If there's such a thing as an unconscious epiphany, I had one.

I clipped the heavy bucktail from the tippet and dropped it into the water. The box of flies that had come with my new outfit contained a pair of small Deceivers, slender patterns tied on size 2 hooks. Too small and too light, according to my companions, but I picked one and tied it to my leader. I'd been using the stripping basket my hosts had given me, but in waist-deep water it was more hindrance than help, so I swung it behind me to get it out of the way.

Although nothing could have made that rod a joy to cast, the smaller, lighter fly made casting considerably less miserable. I'd been imitating the steady, fast retrieve the other guys were using, tucking the rod under my arm and stripping with both hands, but that now struck me as entirely too much work. Besides, none of my companions had hooked a fish. I threw the little Deceiver maybe fifty feet and let it hang in the weak current for half a minute. Then I moved it, slowly, with foot-long strips. After a few strips, I angled the rod off to one side, wondering if the current had enough oomph to put a belly in the line and swing the fly a few feet. It did, barely. I made a few more slow strips, and let the fly hang in the current while I fumbled a cheap cigar out of my pocket and lit it.

This is more like it, I thought. To hell with how these other guys fish. And if the fish don't like it slow and lazy, to hell with them too.

I kept throwing medium-distance casts and retrieving them very slowly. I had several bites before I realized that they were strikes. Little stripers do that sometimes; you feel a soft, tentative tug that comes and goes before your senses understand it, kind of like the bite of a big crappie in cold water.

I shoved the rod tip into the water and stripped slowly. The fly seemed to hang up on something rubbery. I gave the line a quick tug and felt a fish on the other end.

"Art's got one," somebody yelled when he saw my rod come up. Someone else hollered encouragement.

It wasn't much of a striper, maybe fourteen or fifteen inches. But he felt good. I stripped him in, shoved a thumb into his yap, and lifted the little bass from the water.

"Thank you," I said to him, quietly. "You're the only honest player in the whole goddamn business." The fish said nothing. I popped the hook out of his jaw and turned him loose.

"What did you get him on?" someone yelled.

"Little blue and white Deceiver," I said. "Real slow." A couple of guys began studying fly boxes.

I caught three more, one almost identical to the first fish, one genuine runt, and one just big enough that I played him from the reel. All of them fell for the slow retrieve.

It was getting dark. Our guide called a conference. He could take whoever wanted to keep fishing to a sandbar that had good night action, and return whoever didn't want to fish anymore to the inn. I asked to be dropped off at the inn. The other guys wanted to try for bigger fish.

All the other parties were still on the water when I got back to the inn, and I had a solitary drink at the bar. It had been a good evening, I realized. I'd enjoyed the hell out of those four little stripers. Some kind of separation had happened in my mind, and I'd started to climb out of a two-year funk.

The fish are not the problem, I thought. There's nothing wrong with them. Maybe the angling business has its share, and then some, of blowhards and shills and cheap hustlers, and maybe my trade sometimes consists of putting a respectable facade on a cut-rate whorehouse, and perhaps the sport attracts a disproportionate number of self-congratulating snobs, but so what? What does any of that have to do with *my* fishing?

Nothing. Nothing at all, as long as I don't want it to. I sipped my Scotch and thought about how old instincts had taken over, how old pleasures had again felt good. I'd been letting the bad guys win, I realized. Business belongs in the office; I would not let it share the water with me.

The day after I got home, I bought a fishing license. That weekend, my wife and I went to a big reservoir in the mountains and raised hell with rock bass and smallmouths, catching fish until my left thumb was raw from lipping them. The following week, I went trout fishing for the first time in almost two years and caught a couple of wild brookies.

I fished often that summer and autumn, and enjoyed it. The cynicism and burnout and bitterness went away, fading into a sort of amused contempt for the more stupid and seamy aspects of the business that produced my paychecks.

I fished only and exactly as I pleased, never once feeling, as I had felt a few years before, that I *should* try to learn a certain technique or visit a particular place because it was somehow my job to do so. I made little balsa popping bugs and threw them with cheap home-made rods and caught scads of sunfish, and never thought about the article on high-performance saltwater reels I'd edited the day before. After patching up the mangled grammar of a demented screed about ludicrously complex steelhead flies, I'd tie a few crude foam-rubber ants and use them to catch brook trout after work. The funny-looking softshell turtles were still living in the local bass pond, and I was glad to renew our acquaintance. A colleague knew a good small-mouth river a hundred miles to the south; we made the expedition and caught fat bass in water that flows through upscale suburbs populated by golfers. I found new fishing spots close to home, nondescript places where I could be alone and have little adventures like those I'd had as a kid. In time, I rediscovered level-wind reels and plug-casting rods, and the possibilities of my world doubled.

The business of angling assumed its proper place: a way to pay the bills. I would do the best work I could, try hard not to insult the readers with egregious puffery or arrant nonsense, and leave the hype and phony science and empty jargon at the office. My work, the making of fishing magazines, has very little to do with real fishing, or at least with my fishing. In finally reaching that conclusion, I merely joined the wise majority of anglers who do not read angling periodicals.

Maybe I made peace with cynicism, or maybe I pulled off the characteristically masculine trick of putting different parts of life into neat, sealed compartments. I don't care. I relearned, on my own terms, what it is to be a fisherman, and the lessons have been better, sweeter, funnier, and clearer the second time around.

I wrote a good review of that unpleasant rod, then consigned it to a corner of my office. Three years later, I sold it and the reel, and spent the money on a new level-wind reel, a couple of inexpensive plug rods, and a bunch of lures, all of which have served me well.

*Vermont, 2001*

CHAPTER 2

# *The Art of Deception*

BIG, BROWN, LUMBERING MAYFLIES WERE STILL DANCING IN THE AIR and lighting on the little river in northern New Jersey, a fish was still rising about fifty feet upstream in the spot under a bush where God himself couldn't get a good drift, and I still had at least half an hour of light left. But I stepped out of the water and cleaned the two trout I had put in the creel. I kept some fish in those days, before Mary Jo and I were married. I'd race home from the river and call her, then, still smelling of bug dope and fish slime, make the half-hour drive to her place and cook us a late dinner, one fresh trout apiece.

It had been a good evening, and that made it easier to leave before dark. I'd caught four trout, all on complicated, extended-body dry flies tied specifically for this hatch. Maybe I didn't know the scientific name of the mayflies, but I knew what they looked like and how long they drifted on the water, and my imitations had fooled four fish in barely an hour. A nice piece of fly fishing, if I did say so myself, and a vindication of many hours at the vise.

I'd rinsed most of the blood and slime off my hands when I heard footsteps on the gravel path. Two boys on the cusp of their first eruptions of acne, one toting a cheap spinning rod and the other lugging an ancient metal tackle box, approached the spot where I'd been fishing. They said hello and asked about my luck.

I showed them my two dead trout and described the two I'd released. Suitably impressed, the boys asked how I'd caught them. I showed them the dry fly still on the tippet and the soggy one stuck in the fleece patch on my vest.

"They're hittin' on top," the taller boy said to the other. "We gotta use something that floats," he explained, playing Piscator to his friend's Venator.

They opened the tackle box and rummaged through an astonishing assortment of junk, ranging from tarnished June Bug spinners to 6-inch striper plugs made before they, and probably I, were born. I spotted a jar of salmon eggs in the bottom of the box, and another of Uncle Josh's Pork Rind, the lids of both as rusty as the fenders of a car that has spent ten years in the snowbelt.

The taller kid extracted a Hula Popper from the jumble and held it up. It was the three-eighths-ounce model, with a pair of gang hooks, a frog-pattern paint job with a lot of chips and scratches, and a rubber skirt that had seen better days.

"Here we go," the kid said. "This one floats." He tied it to the spinning outfit's line with about seventeen overhand knots, leaving a tag end about an inch long. The line looked heavy enough to jerk a pretty good snook out of a patch of mangroves.

As the leader, the bigger boy rightfully had first crack at the fish, and he stepped onto the big rock where I'd sat to clean my trout. He studied the water for a minute, then seemed to pick a spot downstream and on the far side, where the river ran slowly past a thick stand of cattails. He wound up and fired the plug. The Hula Popper sailed across the stream in a high arc, the cheap, stiff line making a rapid *chick chick chick* sound as it reluctantly peeled off the reel. But the cast was reasonably accurate, if graceless, and the lure landed with a mighty splash about a foot from the cattails. It was not, in my experience, a particularly trouty spot.

Poor kids, I thought. They haven't a clue. Probably fatherless.

The kid let the Hula Popper drift for a couple of feet, then gave the rod a couple of hard yanks. *BLOOP, BLOOP,* the plug went.

Good thing I knocked off early, I thought. That commotion oughtta put down every fish within a hundred yards.

It seemed a shame, because I like to see youngsters catch fish. I decided to stick around. I had a half-formed notion to let the boys waste another few minutes, and then interrupt their exercise in futility to explain, in simple terms, about mayflies and trout feeding on the surface. Maybe I'd let one or both of them try my fly rod. Maybe give them a couple of old flies, just in case one of them could borrow a fly-fishing outfit from an uncle or somebody. Kids need guidance. Without it, they'll get discouraged and give up on fishing.

The boy on the rock made the Hula Popper go *BLOOP* again. Between eruptions, the lure slid across the current on a tight line, kicking up a pretty good wake and frightening a few mayflies off the stream's surface. Intent on the big plug, the boys couldn't see the wise, knowing smile on my mug.

I can't recall ever seeing another trout hit anything with such violence. The strike sounded like one of the boys had whipped a baseball-size rock at the water. A pike would be proud to have made such a splash and swirl.

The kid whooped and reared back, and the two big treble hooks did their job. Another huge splash shattered the stream as the great trout tried to throw the plug. The reel's drag barked once as the fish actually took some of the heavy line, bending the department-store rod double. Then the kid cranked down on the drag knob and started reeling with determination. Had the trout been a ten-pound striper, it still wouldn't have had a chance.

His companion fell on the fish as it slid onto the gravel next to the big rock. He held it in a death grip, teenage fingers shoved up into its gills, and hoisted it aloft.

"Holy shit," someone said. Maybe it was me.

We didn't measure the trout, but I'd guess it was at least twenty inches from nose to tail. A brown, an old hatchery fish that had somehow managed to survive in a grubby little stream and elude dozens of fishermen for a few years after it had been dumped in the river. Its fins and tail looked good, almost like those of a wild fish, and not at all like the ragged, stumpy appendages of the big old breeders that the hatchery guys occasionally release to thrill some suburban fisherman. In eight years of fishing that stretch of that river, I'd never seen a fish like it. I'd never imagined that the water could have held such a trout. It outweighed all four fish I'd caught that evening.

The taller kid, the ringleader, extracted the trebles from the trout's bleeding mouth. His chum, the muscle of the gang, found a sturdy forked stick and shoved one tine up through the fish's gills and out its mouth. He held the trout chest-high, and the three of us stood there looking at it as if we were admiring some kind of pagan battle trophy.

My creel felt less heavy on my shoulder. My mastery of the hatch started to seem like a silly affectation. I resented the two hoodlums' instant, easy, undeserved success.

Tall Boy turned to me and said, "Thanks for the tip."

"Yeah," Shorty agreed. "Good thing you told us they were hittin' on top."

Then one of the little bastards asked if I had a knife so they could gut the fish. I lied and said I'd lost mine in the stream. Damn kids should learn to come prepared, I reasoned.

Then I went home, put my two puny fish in the freezer, and mixed a stiff drink. Nothing wrecks a good evening faster than having your delusions shattered.

These days, I'd probably enjoy the episode of the Hula Popper trout as much as the two boys did. With age, my delusions have changed: they've grown broader, more catholic.

Fly fishing's logic and lore make sense and work perfectly as long as you stay within a closed system and don't spend much time looking at other guys with other kinds of tackle. Once you start paying serious attention to hardware and bait, to spinning outfits and level-wind plug-casting reels, the holy brotherhood begins to seem more like a club for myopics.

We jabber endlessly about hatches and fly patterns and presentations. Some of us perpetrate magazine articles and books dedicated to the proposition that every fish cares as much as we do about the differences between a Catskill pattern and a thorax tie. All the hatch-matchery and fussing over leaders, we assure one another, all the obsession with perfect dead drifts and flies that look just like female emergers with two broken left legs, we tell ourselves, is absolutely necessary for success. Ours is a subtle art of deception.

It certainly is, but mostly we deceive ourselves. Yes, sometimes a size 18 Blue-Winged Olive with a hackle a particular shade of dun will catch trout when a slightly larger, smaller, darker, or lighter fly goes ignored. But that's not true as often as we like to believe it is. For every time a crafty fly fisher dupes trout or bass that no one else can catch, there are a dozen times when an adept bloke with an ultralight spinning rod or a guy who knows how to handle a level-wind outfit—or even some punk with crummy old tackle and the wrongest possible lure—does better. That's been my experience, anyway.

Not that there's anything wrong with believing the mythology of fly fishing. It's a harmless delusion. We don't hurt ourselves or others, including, much of the time, the fish.

But I sometimes wonder why so many fly fishers believe so devoutly. The evidence doesn't support the party line. Sure, you can point to a turgid magazine article in which a fly-fishing luminary explains how after years (maybe decades) of study, he designed his Mid-Hackled Crippled Bent-Abdomen Off-White Dun to replicate a particular stage in the hatch of *Paracleptomaniac insipidii,* and then began catching carloads of trophy trout previously regarded as beyond the skill of mortals. But his screed seems a tad less convincing when you look at twenty-two other magazine articles and nine book chapters devoted to the emergence of *P. insipidii,* each recommending a fly and method that bear scant resemblance to those in the other samples. The fly designer's article loses a little more plausibility if you turn your head and see the guy a hundred yards downstream hauling out fish with a little red-and-white Dardevle spoon. You start to wonder if you should spend so much time trying to decide between one fly dubbed with fur from an Australian possum's crotch and another made with fuzz from the right hip of a spring-killed Norwegian vixen.

And while we fret over the details of tails and wing profile and thorax color, we cheerfully ignore the big *non sequitur:* that a fish will look at two artificial flies and discern differences a diamond grader wouldn't see, and then, twenty seconds later, pass up a real bug to eat a patently bogus one with a curved hunk of steel hanging out of its butt and a piece of plastic string tied to its snoot.

Fly fishers seem particularly devoted to their faith, but all fishermen cling to pet delusions. Read enough bass-fishing magazines and you have to conclude either that all lures catch fish all the time, or that nearly everyone who writes about bass is roughly as honest as a congressman. Anglers differ in degree, not in the basic pathology, swallowing some propositions as innocently as a small bluegill sucks in a McGinty wet fly, and simply ignoring a far larger body of evidence that might knock one's system off the rails. It's a wacky style of thinking, more akin to a peasant's take on religion than the sort of thought that builds rockets and cures diseases.

Why do we do it? For one thing, we're trained to. Selectively analytical angling is good business. Trumped-up complexity sells tackle and magazines. Once you believe that you've got to have a zillion flies or lures, a high-performance rod and line for every occasion, fifty linear feet of fly-tying books, and a sonar unit that will detect the quivering of an alewife's fins ten fathoms below the boat, you're going to spend some dough. That's good for tackle companies, and it lets publishers peddle ad space and subscriptions. The last thing a magazine wants to do is put out a couple of issues that really do explain everything and save you the trouble of reading future numbers.

But the cynical view can't explain all fishermen, or even most of them. If ten years' experience in the publishing game is any indication, at any given time a good 90 percent of the persons who might be reading fishing magazines and books choose not to, a statistic that bolsters my faith in the native intelligence of the species.

The brighter view is that we are willing dupes—not suckers for charlatans and snake-oil peddlers, but people who *want* to create and accept screwy challenges and then meet them, who need to follow a frivolous, narrow, harmless line of thought to its conclusion, who derive genuine happiness from fooling around with feathers and bits of metal and plastic to produce solutions that don't have problems. We don't need hucksters; we can fool ourselves very well, thank you.

Some of it has to do with the nature of sport. Simply catching trout isn't hard. Get on the stream as the sky just begins to brighten and throw around a tiny Rapala, and you'll catch plenty. Creep down to the water's edge after dark and ever so slowly roll a big night crawler along the bottom, and you'll find out that the stream contains more and bigger trout than you thought it did. The best big-trout specialist I ever met fished only with spoiled calf's liver. Fishing for trout loses a good deal of its mystery when you treat them like catfish.

But we need the mysteries so that we can solve them, and so we create them. We wait to fish until the mayflies hatch because a trout that has just eaten three dozen half-inch-long tannish olive things might forget, temporarily, that other things are also good to eat, and so become harder to hook. We craft a lure that looks to us like one of the tannish olive things, and we cast the lure not in the dim, for-giving light of false dawn or the gloaming, but under a bright sky that illuminates the tippet until it looks fat as a clothesline and makes a fly line throw shadows that spook wild creatures. We make it hard to make it good. People who don't fish, or who see only a bunch of meat on a stringer, can't understand that.

Maybe some of it has to do with looking for answers or a little control. The big stuff—love, family, illness, mortality, what passes for success—can get tiring to think about. But if you can reduce the world to matching a Hendrickson hatch, you can manage the uni-verse pretty well for an hour. Add up all the hatches and spinner falls, and then throw in nymphs and baitfish and frogs and leeches and shrimp on the flats, and a guy can stay happily busy dodging ques-tions he can't answer.

Maybe we forget that fishing, like politics, is local. Each of us finds something that works for two weeks in a five-acre pond and thinks that he has uncovered a truth universal and eternal. It makes for good conversations and enough articles to keep editors off the street.

Most of us don't catch as many fish as we'd like to. We can't do much, at least in the short term, about how much time we have for fishing or the quality of the waters in which we cast. We could do something about becoming better at casting and reading water, but that's slow work for most of us. Tinkering with flies and lures and tackle gives us an instant, endless supply of hope.

And maybe it's just plain fun to set ourselves these little problems and then solve them, to create a pleasant system of questions and answers of our own devising. Of course it's artificial and frivolous. So what? So are the World Series, politics, and business.

During the years when I hardly ever fished with anything but a fly rod, I worked out a group of flies for the largemouths in a vodka-clear pond a few miles from home. My bass flies were smaller than most, mostly dark, and built with lots of parts that moved. I favored versions of Rich Osthoff's Soft-Hackle Woolly Worm weighted to swim with their hook points up, black balsa poppers with yellow spots and soft tails built on light-wire Aberdeen hooks, miniature Cockroach tarpon flies, and small, marabou-tailed Deceivers tied with just a little flash. I fished them with lighter-than-average lines and tippets, and over the course of several seasons satisfied myself that my special flies and subtle presentations worked better than anything else I could throw. The pond seemed to have given up its mysteries, thanks to my analysis of its fish and conditions. No one else who fished the pond seemed to have the success I enjoyed. I was quoted in a book as saying that small bugs catch more bass, including the big guys, and that I didn't believe in the big lure–big fish hypothesis.

Then my dad and a friend of his, a guide, took me bass fishing on a big lake in central Florida and knocked my world off its axis. We dragged immense shiners off the upwind side of a big metal-flake bass boat and heaved half-ounce Rat-L-Trap crankbaits off the other. We hammered the fish, particularly with the crankbaits, and I rediscovered how much fun it is to use a plug-casting outfit.

When I got home, I bought a shiny new, narrow-spool Ambassadeur reel and a couple of plug rods. I started buying lures. Then I started making some. I worked hard at educating my thumb, because using a plug rod well gives me so much pleasure—more, even, than casting with a fly rod.

A year later, I was catching more and bigger bass in my pond than I ever had, throwing jointed Jitterbugs or homemade quarter-ounce spinnerbaits. These days, my top lure is a black or charteuse-and-white spinnerbait with a single size 4 Colorado blade and a hand-tied skirt containing thirty-two to forty strands of silicone rubber. One big, round blade, I've determined, works better than two smaller Colorados, and much better than the long, flashy willowleaf blades found on most spinnerbaits. In clear water, I'm convinced, bass prefer a smaller, sparser skirt. I seem to outfish anyone else at the pond. From late April until the end of October, the bass cannot ignore my homemade spinnerbaits. I've figured out the water and designed exactly the right lures for it.

Sure I have.

But when the fishing's slow, sometimes I remember a pair of skinny kids and a beat-up old Hula Popper with rusty gang hooks, a huge trout hanging on a stick, and a thirty-year-old fool with a box of flies that took twenty minutes each to tie. Then I remind myself that I've simply swapped one set of delusions for another.

Two years from now, if we stay in this neighborhood, I'll have determined that *really* the best way to catch those bass is with a Carolina-rigged root-beer-colored plastic worm fished with a medium-weight spinning outfit. I'll have pictures to prove it. Meanwhile, a guy on the opposite bank will conclude that he has enough evidence to write a magazine article explaining why his jointed yellow popping bugs with orange rubber legs catch bass that won't touch anything else. In a brook two miles down the road, a man will congratulate himself on having perfected an articulated-leg cricket pattern that absolutely *makes* trout come to the surface. Three hundred yards upstream from him, around a bend in the river, a visiting angler will note with satisfaction that his special wombat-fur nymphs, complex little flies tied to replicate perfectly the larvae of *Heptagenia alfredo,* catch trout as well in Vermont as they do back home in Michigan. Fortunately, he will not know that the stream he is fishing has never contained a specimen of *H. alfredo.*

And we'll all go home happy, as long as we don't look very far beyond our own rod tips. That's the great thing about angling: it's a mental game.

*Vermont, 2000*

# CHAPTER 3

# *Always Greener*

I HAVE BEEN FLY FISHING IN SCOTLAND, SORT OF. THE EXCURSION had nothing to do with my work as a perpetrator of outdoor journalism. I would never have seen Scotland but for my wife. She worked in the offices of a big, fancy resort hotel in New England for a while, and, as she always does, Mary Jo excelled at her job. Her first year at the joint, she won the Employee of the Year award. At the time, the hotel was allied with another swank resort in Scotland, and Mary Jo's prize was a trip for two to the Scottish operation.

We didn't go right away because we wanted to take our daughters, then eighteen and fifteen. So we saved for a year until we could afford airfare for the four of us and a room for the girls, and then we went to Scotland.

It is a place worth visiting. The country has a loveliness entirely different from anything I've seen on this side of the Atlantic, the people are handsome and friendly, the children are angelically beautiful, the drivers shame us with their skill, the language caresses the ear, the better newspapers make ours look like the rubbish they are, the barmen know how to pour whiskey, the pub owners know how to make fish and chips. On the edge of the Highlands, the evening light has a quality that combines the canyons of the Southwest with the New England coast after a storm. I have not seen any other light like it.

And Scotland has history that makes anything in America seem like this morning's news. We visited castles. *Real castles,* where kings lived and knights clattered around in armor. At St. Andrews, we clambered over the ruins and climbed the steps of a stone tower built a millenium ago. I touched—with my own hands—an ancient stone sarcophagus said to have held the bones of St. Andrew the Apostle, who was with Christ. With *Christ.* We saw places where Robert the Bruce and William Wallace fought. We stood in rooms that were old when James VI of Scotland took the job as James I of England.

We drove, too, or at least I did while Mary Jo and the girls shrieked in terror. They drive on the left side of the road in Scotland, and the roads are very narrow. We rented a tiny Vauxhall hatchback, a car that would almost fit in the trunk of an old Chrysler Imperial, and discovered that unless you make special arrangements in Scotland, you get a rental car with a manual transmission. The stick shift was no problem—I've been stomping on clutch pedals all my life—but keeping on the left side of the skinny roads *and* shifting gears with my left hand used up pretty much all of my concentration, leaving none for watching signs or using turn signals or entering roundabouts in the correct direction. That the roads were not littered with flaming wrecks and mangled bodies is testament to the skill and patience of the Scottish drivers who dodged the weaving, bucking Vauxhall (I tried, repeatedly, to shift gears with the window crank, but it didn't work) that contained a wild-eyed Yank and three screaming women. It was great fun and I'd do it again in a minute, though I'm not sure that the girls would.

I hadn't planned to fish. This was a family vacation, perhaps the last that all four of us would share. Besides, I was coming out of one of my fly-fishing-sucks phases induced by too much work, and I

really had no interest in trying to catch a Scottish trout. Salmon fishing has never held any interest for me, and the Scots have no bass at
which to throw Jitterbugs.

Then, halfway through our vacation, our elder daughter surprised me by asking to go fishing. She hadn't fished in years, hadn't
shown any inclination to. But that's a teenage girl for you. Don't ask
to do something where and when it's free. No—ask in a place where
doing it will cost several princes' ransoms.

But if a dad has any duty, it is to take his kids fishing. So I made
arrangements for Ellie and me to fish with a ghillie on a wee loch (a
pond, where I come from) owned by the hotel.

Not knowing better, we scheduled our outing for Sunday. When we
met Josh, our ghillie, he explained that ancient church laws forbade
fishing for trout or salmon on the Sabbath. Trout, however, means
the native browns. The wee loch was stocked with rainbows from
America, over which ancient church law apparently has no jurisdic-
tion. You can't fish for browns on Sunday, but you can catch the hell
out of those imported jobs with the red stripes. That was the explanation, anyway. And so we went angling in Scotland for fish whose
ancestors came from California.

We suited up with rubber Wellies and waxed-cotton rainproofs,
even though there wasn't a cloud in the sky, and rode out to the
pond (excuse me—*loch*) in a Land Rover with several fly rods
strapped to the roof. The loch was a lovely thing, its dark water
ringed with sedges. Trout dimpled the surface here and there.

Josh turned out to be a paragon. He put his fly boxes at my disposal and took over the instruction and handling of the daughter so
that Dad could wander around and fish for a while. I clumped
around to the far side of the pond (to hell with this *loch* stuff; lochs
are big enough to contain monsters) and began casting. I could hear
Ellie giggling as Josh coached her.

I caught a few trout on a little black wet fly. They were fat, strong, fast beasts that surprised me with their power. One took me into the backing, which no trout had ever done before. I hooked, jumped, and lost one bruiser the size of a steelhead. They seem to know how to raise rainbows in Scotland.

I moseyed back around the pond to try another of Josh's flies. We got to talking. He told me about the angling clubs to which he belonged, groups that made excursions to rivers and lochs in the Highlands, and about his front-yard salmon fishing on the River Tay. He'd killed a twenty-pounder the week before. Caught it on a worm, he confided, and hinted that salmon *flies* were pretty much for tourists. I had no idea if a word of it was true, but I was growing to like the guy.

He asked me where we were from and if I fished much at home. Not enough, I said, but some.

"Do you fish for the black bass?" he asked, keenly interested. That was how he said it: The Black Bass, a fish always introduced with the definite article.

Naturally, I replied. All real Americans do.

"And do you use one of those wee cunning reels with the spool that goes around and around? One of those that you have to work with your thumb?"

I figured that he meant a level-wind baitcaster and told him that I used one often. The educated thumb, after all, is as integral to American culture as the infield-fly rule.

"God, how I'd love to fish for the black bass with one of those reels," Josh said.

Then began a torrent of questions.

Was the purple plastic worm as good as he'd heard?

Sometimes, I said, though black also has its moments, and the garish, metal-flake Culprit Fire and Ice worm is often irresistible to bass in dark water.

Spinnerbaits—did I favor the Colorado or willowleaf blade?

It depends, I told him. For most of my own fishing, I used baits with Colorado blades. But farther south, many anglers find the willowleaf more effective.

Does the black bass really snatch frogs and mice from the shallow fringes of a pond? Does this wonderful fish truly rise with the savage violence he'd heard and read about?

Often enough, I assured him, particularly in the evening. And a grand sight it is.

Back to worms—did I prefer the Texas or Carolina rig?

Texas, I said, but mostly as a function of where and how I fish. In big lakes, expecially in the South, the Carolina rig is often the better choice.

Did I know Roland Martin or Jimmy Houston?

Well, no, I said. America is a pretty big place.

What did I think of reels with magnetic cast control?

They work fine, I allowed, though I have a soft spot for purely mechanical reels like my Ambassadeur and Lew's Speed Spool.

Did I often fish jigs?

Not often, I admitted, though I sometimes use a jighead with a Mister Twister grub on it.

"Ah, the *Mister Twister*," Josh sighed, pronouncing the name as if it were sacred.

Then he explained that he and all his mates watched American bass-fishing shows on the telly and rented every American bass-fishing videotape they could find. He knew all the stars: Roland Martin, Jimmy Houston, Denny Brauer, Hank Parker, Bill Dance, Orlando Wilson.

His dream, he told me, his one great goal as an angler, was someday to fish for the black bass in Lake Okeechobee, using a plastic worm and a level-wind reel that he controlled with an educated, Americanized thumb.

Mind you, this chap lives next to the River Tay. He fishes for Atlantic salmon often, and catches plenty of them. He ties lovely

trout flies and throws a mean fly line. He has caught trout through-
out Scotland and in Wales. He lives in a country of stunning beauty
and belongs to an angling culture far older than mine. Nearly every
week during the season, he and his mates fish for brown trout in
Scottish lochs and Scottish streams.

And he yearns with all his heart to stand on the deck of a bass
boat and drag a plastic worm through the hydrilla in Lake Okeechobee. More than anything in the world, he wants to catch the
black bass.

Well, why not? It's good fishing. And anything you've never
done is exotic.


Ellie hadn't caught a fish yet, so Josh and I stopped palavering and
tried to help her. Ellie's difficulty was that she simply couldn't cast far
enough and quickly enough to drop a fly in front of one of the moving rainbows. She was getting frustrated.

Once again, Josh was a paragon. He tied on a fresh fly—"a wee
black sedge" that looked like one of the bugs that had begun to
hatch—and then backed off so that Dad could be the hero. Ellie and
I took up a spot on the edge of the pond, our feet in the water, and
waited for a fish to approach.

One came cruising along the bank, making a series of dimples as
it sipped the little dark caddisflies from the surface. I explained to
Ellie that we had to anticipate where the fish would be and then
drop the fly right in front of it at just the right moment. It would not
be an easy cast, I said. Maybe I should make the cast, I suggested, and
then give her the rod if the fish took the fly.

She nodded, eager to pull against a fish, and suddenly a nine-
teen-year-old was my little girl again, completely confident that
Daddy would make the fish bite.

So I waited until the riseforms had come close and then began
false-casting, measuring the length of my line against the trout's
progress. The fly dropped about four feet in front of the last rise,

maybe thirty feet away from us. I let it sit for a second and then gave it a gentle twitch. A big, dark snout came to the surface and sucked in the wee black sedge.

*Thank you,* I said to the trout.

I tightened the line to nudge the hook home and handed the rod to Ellie as the rainbow ran. Then she had the fish on the reel, the rod bent way over and the reel making lovely sounds. A couple minutes later, Josh slid his net under a fat, twenty-inch trout. We laid the fish on the grass to take a few pictures, and then Ellie and I put the rainbow back in the dark water.

"That was cool," she said.

"Well done, sir," Josh murmured.

I hope that he catches a fifteen-pound bass in Lake Okeechobee someday, on a black plastic worm rigged Texas style and with all the telefishin' stars watching.

*South Carolina, 2002*

## CHAPTER 4

# *Two Tips from the Pros*

EDITING FISHY PUBLICATIONS HAS NOT AFFORDED ME THE OPPORTU-
nities for travel that most readers would assume it has. I do not spend
three weeks a month at luxurious lodges in exotic destinations or in
camps an hour by float plane from the nearest paved road. Invitations
to such places come my way two or three times a year, but I can
hardly ever spare the time for anything resembling a real fishing trip.
Editing and writing do not pay well enough for a guy with family
responsibilities to relax for, say, five whole days in a row. By and
large, I get my fishing on the run.

But my work has given me the benefit of hundreds of conversations with guides who write for magazines. Many of these chats have
turned to the topic of things that drive guides crazy. Indeed, a pattern emerges from these conversations. Most fly fishers, no matter
how wealthy or well equipped or widely traveled, share certain inad-
equacies and exhibit common shortcomings.

I am not without sin, so please note that I am not casting stones
at fellow anglers. I am merely a vessel, a conduit for the observations
of folks who spend a lot of time on the water and watch a lot of fly

fishers fail to get the job done. You may regard this chapter as secondhand advice. But unless a lot of guides have been conspiring to lie to me for the past decade, it's advice worth listening to.

The most common shortcoming of the average fly fisher is that he simply cannot cast. He can't for several reasons, all of them mental: an inflated view of his own prowess, a consistent failure to listen to his betters, a refusal to practice, and a reflexive tendency to seek answers in the wrong places.

A female friend once asked me if I knew why women make such lousy carpenters. I admitted my ignorance.

"It's because we can't measure," she said, and held up a thumb and forefinger about four inches apart. "All our lives, we're told by men that this is eight inches."

Most fly fishers are men and therefore genetically predisposed to exaggerate length. If you could put a tape measure on the average "sixty-foot" cast that fly fishers talk about, you'd discover that it's actually closer to forty feet. And if you watched enough sixty-foot casters, as guides do, you'd learn that most of them struggle to hit that forty-foot mark consistently and with reasonable accuracy.

Collectively, we suffer from a delusion of competence. It's a rare angler who doesn't think of himself as a competent, adequate, fundamentally sound caster. Odds are that he's actually poor, inflexible, and inefficient. It's not strictly or even mostly a question of distance, though throwing for long yardage sometimes matters very much. Casting well—better, that is, than the average guy—comprises several attributes: efficiency, consistency, and flexibility.

It's easy to test yourself. Take your favorite rod out in the yard and peel off some line. Put a target on the ground thirty-five feet behind you and try hitting it with your backcast. It's not a stunt. Your forward cast depends almost entirely on the quality of your backcast. If you can't produce a tight, fast, straight, accurate loop on the backcast, you're not even in the game. The loops you throw behind you should mirror the best loops you throw in front of you.

Now put a target fifty feet in front of you. Pick up about twenty-five feet of line and, with no more than two backcasts, shoot your practice fly to the target. (You *are* practicing with a fly on the leader, right?) Do it twenty times in a row. No hauling, please; produce all the line speed entirely with your rod hand.

Pinch a split shot onto the leader in front of the practice fly and repeat both drills, adjusting your casting stroke and loop as necessary to deal with the extra weight. Then take off the practice fly and sinker and tie on a cork popping bug one size larger than you'd normally expect to cast with your outfit. Repeat both tests.

Ring up a fishing buddy and have him come over with several rods of various lengths, weights, and actions, none of which you've ever used. See how quickly you can adjust to each of your friend's outfits.

Do all of these things with the wind behind you, in your face, and from each side.

If you can pass all the tests, give yourself a pat on the back. Congratulations: you've become pretty good at the baby stuff. You're ready to *begin* learning some of the trickier aspects of fly casting, now that you have a grasp of the rudiments. And rudiments are precisely what we've been testing. Advanced casting is when the guide says, "Permit—two o'clock—eighty feet—*now*," and with no more than two backcasts, you drop a size 1/0 crab fly on a target the size of a dinner plate in front of the fish nine rod lengths away, allowing perfectly for the ten-knot wind blowing from your right side. (No, I can't do that. But I know guys who can.)

If you can't pass the tests, admit that you're a duffer and get to work. Welcome to a big club. Spend some money on casting lessons and books; forgo the new rod or reel if you have to. And for Christ's sake, *pay attention*. When an instructor or author who can hit the permit at eighty feet keeps hammering away at the rudiments, don't say, "Well, yeah, I understand that, but . . ." There's no *but* to it. Everything depends on accelerating the rod to the necessary speed, moving it in a straight line, and stopping it dead. Until you can *do* those things over and over again, making adjustments for the length of line, the length or action of the rod, the wind, and the size or weight of the fly, you simply aren't casting. You're not even ready to begin learning.

The rudiments, and even the tricky stuff, are eminently learnable as long as you're willing to practice. That's where most of us guarantee our failure. We don't practice our casting, or we don't practice the right things. Professional athletes, men and women gifted with inherently superior bodies, train and practice every day just to maintain skills that they've already repeated hundreds of thousands of times. Yet a paunchy, middle-aged fly fisher blithely assumes that he can go three months without touching a rod and then somehow perform a fairly complicated physical stunt like double-hauling seventy feet of line into the teeth of a gale. The wonder is that guides are not all alcoholics.

Even with disciplined practice, improvement comes slowly. I speak from experience. You have to think in terms of months, or even years, rather than hours and days. So what? One of the beauties of angling is that even a paunchy, middle-aged guy can get better at it.

As often as not, the bloke who hasn't picked up a rod in three months will go fishing, cast poorly, and begin shopping for a new rod. It's human nature: blame the tool. The rod usually has nothing to do with the problem or the solution. Yes, it's possible to have a genuinely bad rod; I've owned a few. And there's no question that some rods will let you cast a little farther than others will. But the quality of your casting begins and ends in your rod hand. If you cannot cast well with an entry-level, hundred-dollar rod chosen at random in the local tackle shop, then you need more lessons and practice. Every expert caster and guide I know agrees with that notion. You cannot buy tighter loops and greater accuracy. You have to make them. By hand.

No sane person would expect that merely buying a Steinway would automatically make him a concert pianist. Yet the first instinct of many fly fishers is to attack their casting deficiencies by buying new rods.

Leaders, too, get blamed for poor casting. While a grotesquely wrong leader can fail to perform, turnover problems almost always come from poor casting. As a trout-fishing guide once remarked to me, "If you really know how to cast, the leader doesn't much matter." This gent uses fairly soft, slow bamboo rods that do not produce supersonic line speeds. He still has no trouble turning over long leaders, to the design of which he pays little attention. He can cast.

But we love to look for answers in the wrong places, and so we fret endlessly over leader tapers and materials. I'll depart from the wisdom of guides for a minute and offer a few of my own observations. First, check the butt of the leader. Its stiffness must not exceed that of the fly line. If the end of the fly line bends more easily than the butt of the leader does, you will have problems. Second, check the taper of an extruded, knotless leader. Just pull the thing between your fingers to feel how quickly the diameter decreases. If the butt becomes noticeably thinner within just a few feet, as some of them do, try a different brand of leader. Third, cut off the first six inches of a fly line before rigging it. Nearly all lines have a skinny, level tip from six to twelve inches in length. Cut it off, and you'll find that your casts turn over with more authority.

If your leader's butt section is not stiffer than the end of the fly line, and if the butt maintains its diameter for, say, three feet before the material starts to become thinner, and if you still have trouble getting the leader to straighten, then you should look first to your casting. Experimenting with six dozen different leader formulas probably won't solve the problem. Casting instruction and diligent practice probably will.

On the other hand, though, making up six dozen different leaders will at least give you some knot-tying practice, and that brings us to the average angler's second shortcoming: he ties bad knots. There's hardly any excuse for this, since tying good knots doesn't require talent or physical skill. All you have to do is park your rump in a comfy chair and dedicate some time and monofilament to the job.

"He broke me off!" is just another projection of blame. In most cases, it's more accurate to admit that you failed to make a good knot, and so gave the fish something that was very easy to break.

Don't believe me? Try this. String up your 6-weight rod. Remove the leader and attach the fly line to a reasonably accurate scale. Have a friend hold the scale while you back up thirty or forty feet. Try to generate an honest four pounds of pull on the scale with your 6-weight fly rod. But don't try too hard, because that fancy trout rod might blow up before the scale hits the four-pound mark. With an 8- or 9-weight rod, try to produce eight pounds of pull. You probably can't.

Some years ago, I had the chance to assist in a demonstration by a legendary saltwater angler. We used a fiberglass 12-weight tarpon rod, a fearsome club the instructor had no fear of breaking. He attached the fly line to a scale, which I held while half a dozen students took turns pulling on the rod. With the rod upright, in the classic (and generally incorrect) fish-playing position, none of the students could produce nine pounds of pull. The biggest guy, who weighed almost three hundred pounds, got the scale to a bit over eight pounds, but he couldn't maintain it. When it was my turn, I managed a hair over six pounds of pull—while straining my guts out with a big-game fly rod.

Then the angling legend showed us how to use a heavy fly rod to fight a big fish, and we all did a little better. With the rod held low and to the side, most of the students managed, with lots of grunting, to get the scale almost to the ten-pound mark and keep it there. The big guy briefly generated about fifteen pounds of pressure, enough to pull me off balance. I was able to maintain about nine pounds on the scale, again while straining as hard as I could.

The point is that with proper technique and an expert coach at my elbow, I, a very fit thirty-year-old at the time, could generate only nine pounds of pressure with an exceptionally tough, powerful fly rod. With a freshwater rod (anything up through a 7-weight, say) and average fish-fighting technique, a typical fly fisher probably never produces three pounds of strain on a tippet. Remember that a fish in the water weighs very little or nothing. Ten pounds of relentless pressure will whip a hundred-pound tarpon, according to the expert who gave the demonstration. It's worth noting that many saltwater anglers have gone ten-to-one; that is, they've landed or boated a hundred-pound fish with ten-pound line, eighty-pound fish with eight-pound line, and so forth.

Modern tippet material is strong stuff. Some 6X materials have breaking strengths (according to the labels) of more than three and a half pounds. Even the cheap 3X material I use for bluegill fishing has a nominal strength of seven pounds.

So why do fly fishers break off fifteen-inch trout? Bad knots seem an obvious reason. Most of the guides with whom I've discussed the subject agree. Quite a few of them are endlessly amazed and exasperated by their clients' refusal to learn anything about knots and rigging. Some of them tie on a client's fly without asking or being asked, having learned to assume that a customer left to his own devices will unfailingly produce a one-pound knot with six-pound line.

"People show up with three thousand dollars' worth of rods and reels," one friend told me, "and pay me four hundred bucks a day to go fishing, and they have *no clue* how to tie a fly to the goddamn leader. So I get to spend half the day jumping off the poling platform to tie on their flies and fix their leaders instead of looking for fish, which is what they think they're paying me for."

It's baffling, because there's no end of books and articles about knots and rigging. You can probably find all the information you need at a public library. It's not as if you need to learn six different knots for every application. Nor do you have to worry whether one knot will test 0.03 percent stronger than another, because the difference between two correctly tied knots is rarely as great as the difference between well-made and poorly tied specimens of the same knot. You need to learn how to tie and when to use a total of maybe half a dozen knots, and then practice them until you can make them perfectly in poor light. It is not an insurmountable challenge.

No guide has ever told me that he wished that his clients tied more flies, knew more about entomology, had a better grasp of fly-fishing buzzwords, or owned more high-end reels with disk brakes slightly better than those on the average European sports car. Many guides, indeed, dismiss a client's obsession with fly patterns as a distraction, an irrelevancy. In the great, eternal pattern-versus-presentation argument, they come down with both feet on the side of presentation. And good knots.

A cynic might point out that guides fish with people who *need* guides, and therefore develop a pessimistic view of anglers. But a lot of good anglers also fish with guides, and the world is full of inept anglers who never hire a guide.

It might be true that guides fish with a lot of men who can afford to hire a guide for every fishing trip. Affluent types often exhibit an interesting and contradictory mentality. They hold dear the American belief that money makes you smart. At the same time, they believe that having money liberates them from having to know things. The wealthy can pay people, including guides, to know things for them. And they can buy solutions to most of their problems. So, maybe guides do develop a somewhat unbalanced view of fly fishers.

But when I look around me at a fishing show or on the water, and when I look behind myself at my own backcast, I can't help feeling that my guide friends are right. The secret to hooking more fish and losing fewer is not tying more and more complex flies or buying more rods or switching to another brand of miraculous leader material. Learn to throw a good line that has a good knot at the end, and your guide suddenly becomes a whole lot better at his job. And happier.

*South Carolina, 2002*

CHAPTER 5

# What I Learned at Camp

SOME YEARS AGO, I GOT TO SPEND A FEW DAYS AT A TONY SALMON camp on private water in Canada, the sort of camp that has employees whom the guests refer to as houseboys. For lunch, the chef prepared lobster or better. The supply of top-shelf liquor seemed endless, and though we sports shared a shower, we had plenty of towels laundered and neatly folded by the houseboy or some other minion. The plates and glasses were considerably nicer than those I use at home. It was not the sort of fish camp to which you need to bring your own stringer or bait bucket, or even your own bottle of single-malt Scotch.

I was there by invitation, and I suspect as a sort of trained monkey. A big, wealthy publishing company, which at the time owned the piddling little outfit for which I toiled, used the camp for a couple of weeks every summer to entertain important advertising clients, mostly from the *shmatte* trade. In other words, the executives of a prosperous, trendy magazine would blow the executives of certain clothing companies to a few days of salmon fishing and drinking at a swank lodge, just so the boys could bond and maybe chat about business. It's how you build relationships in the glamorous world of media. Any resemblance to rewarding a customer for spending his company's money with your company is purely coincidental, I'm sure.

I had nothing to do with the magazine underwriting the outing, barely knew the top executive acting as host, and had never met anyone else in the group with which I spent several days. My interest in Atlantic salmon fishing borders on zero, and I have no appreciation of the salmon-fishing culture, much of which strikes me as a textbook example of the ruling class at play. I was invited at the last minute, after a cancellation. Maybe the guy who invited me was just being generous, or maybe he wanted to get to know me better, since we were, in a sense, working for the same outfit. Or maybe, as I suspect in uncharitable moments, he thought it would be nifty to bring along a real, live outdoor editor, a backwoodsman who wore flannel shirts to work and actually knew about manly stuff like tying knots and paddling a canoe and gutting a fish. His other guests, the important ones with big advertising budgets, might get a kick out of spending a few days with a rustic type. Might give them good stories to tell in the bar at the country club. But I feel that way only in uncharitable moments.

The gang met at a small airport in suburbia and took a private turboprop to a much smaller airport in northern Maine. A van from the lodge carried us across the border into Canada. During the trip, I quickly twigged that I was way, way out of my element. I surmised at once, for instance, that none of the other lads had driven to the airport in a ten-year-old pickup with rust holes in its sides and a balky transmission. And though the topic of home improvement never came up, I got the impression that none of my companions made it a habit to fix his own pipes, wire his own closet lights, or split firewood to keep the oil bill down.

Not that they weren't nice guys. The wealthy are usually pleasant companions. They have good manners and they don't smell. They're good at breezy chatter and quick to laugh.

My new friends' clothing puzzled me for a while. I was dressed in my fishing togs, the sort of duds most people wear for raking leaves or painting the house: bindlestiff couture, as I call it. Everyone else on the plane, except the two young guys flying it, sported designer-label casual wear that editors of fishing rags can't afford. Then it dawned on me that these boys were simply wearing their products, or at least the products of the women working in their Mexican factories.

At the airport in Maine, a strip of decrepit tarmac surrounded by pine forest, I chatted with the pilot and copilot, both in their early twenties. They had to stick around in case one of our captains of industry had to rush back to civilization to attend to business, so they had made plans for the next three days. They had rented a cabin on a nearby lake and brought an impressive assortment of liquor that they planned to share with a couple of French Canadian whores they'd lined up for the duration. They'd also brought a couple of spinning rods, in case they wanted to fish. I sensed they were in for a better time than I was.

On the van ride to camp, my new companions talked of branding and image building, occasionally straying from business to swap golf tips. I pretended to care and watched the endless forest roll by. We drove over a few little streams that looked like good brook-trout water, but since no one else seemed to notice, I kept my thoughts to myself.

We led an enviable life at camp. The chef and houseboy had a huge breakfast waiting for us as we tumbled from our bunks. We fished for a few hours in the morning, each with his own guide who managed a big freighter canoe equipped with an outboard motor, then returned to the lodge for a lunch that would shame the dinners provided at some four-star hotels. After lunch, we relaxed and digested for a spell. A few of the guys went jogging to work off lunch; I gave casting lessons to those interested. Then we hit the water again for a few hours, returning to camp at a decent hour for cocktails. My fellow sports devoted the evenings to serious drinking, tales of business or sexual exploits, and making fun of the guides, none of whom seemed to own any designer clothing. Most of the guides, in fact, had wardrobes even shabbier than mine, and their outfits, accents, and bad teeth provided endless merriment for my comrades.

The drought that had withered New England that year was even worse in eastern Canada, and the river was low, as warm as a small-mouth stream, and very clear. A few salmon lay in the bottoms of pools, gasping for oxygen. Later, I heard stories of a big fish kill in the main river downstream. The guides worked hard, but the fishing was dismal. One of the guests, the CEO of a big clothing company, killed a salmon in a pool downstream of the lodge, and I landed a grilse after my guide hooked it and insisted that I take the rod. I hope it was not representative of *Salmo salar;* if it was, give me a channel catfish any day. Early one evening, I wandered far upstream from my guide and used my light rod and a big wet fly to catch a couple of long, skinny brook trout in a riffle. They were poor excuses for trout, not at all like the fat, snotty, vibrantly colored brookies I was used to catching, but they seemed more legitimate than an immature salmon hooked by another guy, and I was glad to catch them. The other five guests had a long visit to Skunksville.

During and after lunch, most conversation concerned the business of selling clothing and men's fragrances to yuppies. It might have been more interesting, at least for me, to palaver with the guides, but they dined separately, on hot dogs.

Still, the afternoon conversations were illuminating. I'd had no idea that grown, heterosexual men could spend hours talking about the ad campaign for this or that fragrance, or that anyone regarded the Ralph Lauren Polo campaign as one of the major accomplishments and turning points of Western civilization. But my companions could and did. For the first hour on the first day, it was interesting to listen to, much as the conspiracy theories of a monomaniac are fun for a while. By the third day, I understood why these guys were rich and why I will never be.

The epiphany came on the second afternoon. After lunch, I gave a casting lesson to the *shmatte* magnate who'd caught a salmon, and his "creative guy" who handled advertising and image building watched us. Over drinks back inside the lodge, the creative guy—let's call him Kyle, since that's usually what they're called—expressed an interest in my work. What was it like, he wanted to know, to edit a fishing magazine? How did I position it in the marketplace so as to establish a unique brand identity to appeal to the fly-fishing lifestyle?

I hadn't thought about my job in quite those terms, and the question baffled me. There wasn't much positioning involved, I explained. I put out a practical, how-to magazine. People who fish like to catch fish. My job was to look for articles that might help them catch a fish or two, and then flog the articles into a semblance of correct, clear, and lively English.

But, Kyle wanted to know, how did I *position* the magazine relative to competitors? What was the marketing strategy in terms of identity and lifestyle?

Well, none, I admitted. I found and edited pieces about reading water and tying flies and making good casts. People who want to catch fish with a fly rod need to know such things. Ain't no positioning to it, I allowed. I printed useful stuff that folks could understand and, I hoped, enjoy reading.

Kyle thought for a second while he sipped his Scotch. "Okay, I think I get it," he finally said. "You position it as authentic."

*Position it as authentic.* And, instantly, I understood everything wrong with the modern world, everything the Communists had meant by the term "decadence." Inwardly, I wept for the civilization bequeathed to us by Aristotle and Newton, for the legacy of Washington and Lincoln.

Then I gave up and pretended that I needed to visit the toilet. You cannot have a serious conversation with a man who uses such language. You just can't. That evening, I drank more than I should have, but probably less than I needed to.

The next day, as we drifted down the river smoking cheap cigars after I suggested that we give up on the fishing, my guide paid me a great compliment. "That's some bunch of filthy rich cocksuckers you're stuck with, eh?" he said.

Our pilots were a sorry sight when we met them at the airstrip in Maine, bleeding from the eyes and looking like they'd aged a decade in a few days. Clearly, the combination of abundant booze and a brace of Canuck hookers had lived up to its promise. They'd done no fishing. But I bet they came home from the North Woods feeling cleaner than I did.

*South Carolina, 2002*

## CHAPTER 6

# A Taste
# of Virtual Blood

THE FIRST EIGHT TROUT CAME SO EASILY THAT I KNEW SOMETHING was wrong. Everyone has days when his casts unroll perfectly to hit targets smaller than his reel, when he chooses flies with infallibility that would make a pope jealous. But I'm never so sharp that I can hook eight trout in ten casts from the same spot. After releasing number eight, I paused to study the situation.

We'd had a couple weeks of warm, dry weather after opening day, and the smaller streams had late-June water by the beginning of May. The early hatches—Quill Gordons and some little gray mayflies whose name I don't know—actually came off on time and in good numbers. A fishable Hendrickson hatch seemed likely. It was a good spring to be a trout fisherman.

But anybody can play the percentages. I'd taken the morning off to see if the unseasonable weather had awakened the panfish a few weeks earlier than normal. A new season doesn't seem truly started until I catch the first few sunfish. And so I had begun the day at a little lake in a not-yet-open state park, walking the shoreline and casting a wet fly wherever I had room. Naturally, it was a bust. A few weeks of nice April weather do not erase a New England winter. I caught one frigid pumpkinseed that came to my hand with barely a wiggle and felt like a fillet fresh from the freezer.

By nine o'clock I was driving to the office. A fast-food joint on the main drag beckoned with the prospect of a life-giving infusion of grease, salt, and coffee. I ordered a large coffee, and that made all the difference. With half of it undrunk after the oleaginous meal had slid down my throat, I went outside to stroll down the side street. There's a stream behind the fast-food place, and I figured I'd look at the water while finishing my coffee.

A footbridge, the abutments of which once supported a span for cars and trucks, crosses the stream at the end of the side street. Beneath the bridge, an old concrete spillway creates a long, almost perfectly rectangular pool upstream and a fifty-foot chute of fast water downstream. Below the chute, the little river spreads out into a long pool with easy wading and plenty of casting room on one side and a deep, dark trough on the other. I walked halfway across the bridge and looked at the downstream pool while I sipped my coffee. For April, the water looked very good. I wished I'd brought my sunglasses.

A fish rose. Another made a dimple five yards downstream. I thought I saw a third rise close to the riprap on the deep side, where the fast water starts to slow down.

Maybe I'd better catch one of those fish, I thought. Just to see if they're trout or chubs. It's not like I'm playing *extra* hooky, I reasoned; no one at the office *expects* me before lunchtime. Rigorous training in applied logic often comes in handy.

So I walked back to the car, donned hip boots, strung up the little fiberglass 4-weight, and tied on a small bunny-fur nymph ribbed with Krystal Flash. It's as good a fly as any to start with. I clipped my flip-up shades to my glasses, but left them flipped up for the walk down to the stream.

A wide, flat gravel bank on the shallow side of the pool makes it easy to sneak down to the tailout without spooking the fish. As I waded shin-deep into the tailout, I saw that a couple of fish were working in the middle of the pool; not regularly, the way trout do in the middle of a serious feed, but frequently enough to provide targets.

The little rabbit-fur nymph had drifted perhaps three feet when the line twitched. I lifted the rod and a fish pulled the tip back down. Very cool. As I slipped the ten-inch rainbow back into the stream, I congratulated myself on tying such excellent flies and making such good casts. It's not everybody who can wade into a river and hook a trout on the first cast.

The next nine casts hooked seven more trout—mostly rainbows, with a couple of browns—and I started to understand that neither flies nor casting had anything to do with it. I let the line trail in the current behind me and finally flipped down the polarizing shades.

I do not have good eyes for trout. Bass and sunfish and crappies I can see fine, even in bad conditions. Better than most anglers, I can spot a pickerel hiding in the weeds. But trout, for some reason, are like bonefish to me—invisible until spooked. Even after a lifetime of fishing for them, I almost never see one before it takes my fly.

I guess that's why I hadn't noticed that the bottom of the pool was paved with fish. Or maybe there were too many for any one to stand out from the background. But the polarizing shades made them visible—dozens of trout spread across the gravel in the shallow water, more in tightly packed groups holding in front of and behind rocks in the stronger current, a bunch more darting in and out of the shadows on the deep side. Scads of them, in a pool barely twice as long as my best cast with the short, fiberglass 4-weight.

And not another fisherman in sight.

It wasn't hard to see what had happened. Starting at the spillway, the little river gets stocked a couple times a year. Generally, the hatchery lads do a good job of spreading out the fish, planting most of them farther downstream where a road parallels the river and provides plenty of access. This time, the stocking crew must have suffered a lapse of ambition, and they'd dumped the whole springtime load off the footbridge, filling a single pool with thirty times as many fish as it should have or could possibly support.

Well. Isn't this interesting, I thought. Nobody else around. And no one at the office expects me till maybe one o'clock. At the earliest.

There was only one thing to do. I fished.

Hundreds of dumb, hungry hatchery fish make it easy to exercise a high grade of sportsmanship. One can afford to take chances, to make the game more difficult. I replaced the never-fail nymph with a Hendrickson dry and sent it on its way. After five fish, it no longer floated, and a Light Cahill took its place. The Cahill became too slimy to float after four trout, and I replaced it with a foam-rubber ant, size 14. After a dozen trout, I got bored with the ant and tied on an emerger, a new pattern with a foam wing case that held the fly suspended in the surface film. After ten or twelve fish ate the emerger, I concluded that I had scientific proof that my new design worked just fine, so I knotted a Grizzly Riffle Fly to the tippet.

The Grizzly Riffle Fly is an uncommonly rugged, buoyant pattern, but even it refused to remain afloat after seven or eight trout had chewed on it. I went back to the nymph for a quarter of an hour, then added a couple feet of tippet material and started pitching a soft-hackle wet fly upcurrent. When that lost its novelty, I finally took a few steps upstream and tried a Deer Hair Caddis. The fish ate it, even after it no longer floated.

And so it went. Lord only knows how many trout I caught— however many a man can catch in three hours of steady casting if he pauses only to change flies or add tippet and never makes more than three consecutive casts without hooking a fish. Fifty? Certainly. Eighty? Perhaps. A hundred? The number is not impossible.

I gave up out of fatigue. And because the large coffee had long since worked its way through my kidneys, and if I didn't get to the men's room in the fast-food joint I was going to embarrass myself.

A few fish were still rising in the broken water at the head of the pool. I wished them well.

Later, at the office, I called a friend in Colorado to tell him about my day. John is twice the trout fisherman I am and a much better fly tier. He has a keen sense of the absurd, particularly in fishing.

"I've got this trout-fishing thing figured out," I said. "It's not such a big deal. Forget about hatches and presentations and eight-X tippets and all that crap. All you gotta do is find where the hatchery guys dumped all the fish."

"What happened?" John asked. "What did you do now?"

So I told him about the morning. He laughed and said, "Good for you," a couple times as I jabbered about the dozens of trout I'd caught two hundred yards from a hamburger emporium.

"You need a day like that every now and then," he said. "Hell, you're *entitled* to a few days like that in your life."

"I guess so. Not that I'm proud of it. It's not like it was hard fishing. After a while, I started to feel, I don't know, kinda piggish. But it was fun—most of it, anyway."

"I know," John said. "Once you get that taste of blood in your mouth, it's hard to stop."

He was right. Every one of those trout had gone back into the stream, but the morning had nonetheless been a slaughter, an exercise in mayhem, and that's why it had felt good. You *should* have a day like that every few years. The days of fifty easy fish get you through the lean times. They average out all the days when the fish's cunning exceeds your own, and vindicate the hundreds or thousands of hours spent tying flies and building rods and making leaders. Although we all need the fishing more than we need the catching, each of us does need a spot of wholesale catching once in a while. And sometimes you do need the taste of blood in your mouth, even if you don't shed any.

Such days, though, aren't quite real. They leave unsatisfied something that needs satisfying; they fail to scratch one of the angler's itches.

That evening, I knocked off work an hour before sunset and went back to the stream, but not to the Pool of Plenty. I parked next to a bridge that crosses one of the branches a few hundred yards above the junction pool where the little river's headwaters come together.

As the trout swims, the bridge over the branch is less than a mile from the scene of the morning's carnage. If you don't dawdle, you can fish from the spillway under the footbridge up to the junction pool in less than two hours. At the junction pool, the main river ends and an entirely different world begins. Two worlds, actually. The left branch, the one that runs behind the town's older, more dilapidated strip mall, bounces down a steep gradient, splashing over slabs of bedrock and through rocky chutes from one small, deep pool to the next. Except during floods, its water is always perfectly clear. It holds a lot of native brookies and a few wild browns, and it's one of the few places in these parts with a good population of golden stoneflies.

The right branch, which runs through the downtown area and eventually under the bridge where I'd parked, almost always has some color, even during low water. It flows down a gentler slope, over a bed of gravel and loose, broken rock, and after leaving the moribund business district, through thick woods bordering some older housing tracts. It, too, contains mostly brook trout and a smattering of browns. It also contains a lot of fallen trees and a fair amount of junk: tires, hunks of waterlogged plywood, pieces of fence, and at least one engine block complete with head and manifolds. A friend with whom I sometimes fish the branch named it the Little Shithole. But it's a wild place, despite the trash.

Every step on the loose, slimy rocks is an adventure, and after two hours of wading, your feet and ankles feel like they've been beaten with hammers. Your backcasts have to be accurate and low, since most of them have to go under and between overhanging branches. It's best if they unroll upside down. If you make any noise stumbling into the foot of a pool, you will see a couple of wakes disappearing into the broken water at the head. The fish in the branch don't come from a truck.

The ankle-deep riffle above the bridge where I'd parked rarely holds any fish, and I sloshed through it to reach the first pool, which almost always contains at least two trout. I've seen their wakes dozens of times. One tree lies across the tail of the pool, victim of a flood that undermined its roots, and another, still alive, leans from the opposite bank. Even a sidearm, upside-down backcast is out of the question. The only approach is to climb over the trunk on the left side of the stream and creep up until you just have room to roll-cast, first to the center of the pool, then to the head.

A small trout in the middle of the pool rose to my second cast. I felt him for a second before he came unstuck. Maybe he spooked the other fish in the pool when he bolted; another half dozen roll casts didn't draw a strike.

I reeled in and slogged upstream through some treacherous water where I always come within a hair's breadth of falling in, and reached the first pool where you have room for a real backcast, as long as you keep it short and low. It's an easy pool to overlook the first time you fish the Little Shithole, just a long depression in the riverbed without a well-defined riffle at either end. But the water comes up to my thigh in the deepest part, and the little pool usually holds a brace of fish.

One of them rose to my Grizzly Riffle Fly on the first cast. I saw the flash as the brookie came up and took the fly, grabbing it and turning for the bottom in a single blur of movement. You don't have to set the hook with these fish; just lift the rod tip to get the slack out of the line, and let the trout's movement do the rest.

The soft fiberglass rod jiggled in my hand as the brookie darted around the pool. Our little native trout fight with neither intelligence nor strength, but with a thrashing panic that quickly exhausts them. Even if our wild brookies grew to three times their average size, they'd still be mediocre game fish, less cunning and muscular than largemouths, not so quick and acrobatic as smallmouths.

But they do their best, and my little trout wiggled back and forth across the pool, looking for an escape from the strange pressure in the side of his yap. I stripped him in, half a yard at a time, while he wiggled and thrashed, and slid him into my left hand.

The light was beginning to fail. It had assumed the golden tint we usually don't see until later in the season. Maybe the angle of the light was just right, or maybe my eyes were perfectly adjusted to the twilight gloom of the little pool, but the brook trout, all seven inches of him, lit up as I cradled his body in my hand, the stripes on his fins perfectly distinct from one another, the spots on his sides glowing like fluorescent jig paint. Like most wild brookies, he had a big mouth and teeth larger than you'd expect to see in a small trout.

"Well, don't *you* feel silly," I said to the fish. "Thought that was a real bug, huh?"

The barbless hook came easily out of the side of the brookie's jaw. I opened my hand and the trout slid back into his world, thumping my shin as he rushed away.

Another one rose, gently, at the top end of the little pool. I looked at my fly, looked at the water, and shrugged. All the itches had been scratched. I reeled in and sloshed back to the car.

*Vermont, 1999*

CHAPTER 7

# *Fishing School*

A WHILE BACK, MY FATHER SENT ME TWO PICTURES MY GRAND-
father took at Paulinskill Lake in 1948, when Dad was fourteen. In
the photos, Dad's holding a largemouth bass with one hand and a fly
rod in the other. My grandmother, who passed away when I was a
boy, is in the background, sitting in a chair on the lawn of the cabin
my grandfather bought that year.

The note in which the photos were wrapped says, "The rod is
gone. It was a Horrocks-Ibottson 9-foot, 3-piece bamboo POLE.
The reel is recognizable as a Shakespeare automatic—still in service
and last used on the new Orvis rod you sent." In our family, we hold
on to tackle.

I remember that reel from my childhood. I remember liking the
way it sounded, the mystery of its mechanism, how it made a popping bug scoot when I pulled the lever. When I was a kid, Dad used
that reel on a Heddon Pal rod, a heavy, fiberglass buggy whip with a
soft tip and a spring-loaded reel seat. I rewrapped the rod for him a
few years ago. It might be old and heavy and soft in the tip, but to us
it was worth keeping.

I remember sitting in the bow and listening to Dad fly-casting behind me. The sounds of fly-fishing—the soft *bloop* of a popper, the swish of line passing through the guides—have for me always been among the chief pleasures of this sensuous sport.

We fished a lot at Paulinskill when I was a boy. We had a Starcraft aluminum boat with a blue Evinrude outboard and a red gas tank too heavy for me to lift, and we used to go up the lake early in the morning before the mist burned off, dodging the stumps and snags that were invisible to everyone but Dad, who ran the lake for more than twenty years and never broke a shear pin. To this day, the smell of two-stroke exhaust takes me back to childhood.

The bridge at the lake's waist was high enough that we could pass under it without ducking, but farther up, after we entered the river, we would go under a low wooden bridge and had to scrunch down in the boat. Barn swallows built nests under both bridges, and big yellow-and-black spiders made huge webs where the spans met the abutments. We used to hide under one of the bridges when we got caught in a downpour.

After the second bridge, we entered the magic land we called "upstream." I caught my first trout up there, when I was three years old. I fished upstream with a cane pole, and later with a push-button spincast outfit, and later still with the Garcia ultralight spinning rod I still have.

In the spring, suckers ran upstream and filled the river. Sometimes we saw giant carp; I remember one bumping against the bottom of the Folbot kayak we had for a while. Dad, my grandfather, and I once took the kayak as far upstream as we could. I sat amidships while the men dragged the boat through riffles until we ran out of river. Lewis and Clark never had such adventures.

Upstream, we always looked for a fish we called The Grandaddy Bass, a beast we knew weighed at least ten pounds. We never caught him, but he was a hell of a big fish. We knew. We did catch plenty of small bass and big bluegills and rock bass with bright red eyes. In the spring, when the state stocked the river, we caught trout. We used to see trotlines, ropes suspended from Clorox-jug floats beneath which hung baited hooks. I remember Dad telling me never to disturb a trotline: fishing was fun for us, but the farmer who set the trotline did so to feed his children.

We fished off the dock at the cabin, too. Mostly, my father and grandfather caught carp from the dock, using a secret doughball recipe Dad still hasn't given me. Dad used to slip-cast doughballs with a cheap fly rod equipped with an Ocean City Viscoy reel that had neither a drag nor room for backing. He caught some big carp with that rig, learning how to play strong fish on simple tackle, and learning that sometimes you just have to jam your fingers into the spool and endure the pain. I have the Viscoy now, and don't imagine that I'll ever own a better fly reel.

Mom says that when I was little, I would stand on the dock for hours, contentedly fishing with a lure from which she had removed the hooks. I don't remember that, but I do recall Mom teaching me to tie flies on pieces of paper clips because I was too little to be trusted with real hooks. I recall my first shot of whiskey, which my grandfather poured for me in the cabin at Paulinskill after he, Dad, and I came in from fishing in the rain. And, though I couldn't have been more than three at the time, I remember the first time I held a largemouth bass by the lip. Dad told me that the bass wouldn't wiggle if I grabbed it by the lower jaw. He was right. He's always been right about fish.

Later, when I was bigger, we fished in other places. I remember a morning on Little Swartswood Lake when a twenty-six-inch pickerel grabbed my yellow Rebel plug no more than a yard from the gunwale of our big Grumman canoe. On another morning, we found an immense snapping turtle so old that the moss on its back was as long as a woman's hair. We poked at it with the canoe paddles.

It bit one, leaving a deep scar in the wood. Maybe that morning is why I've never been comfortable in a belly boat. I still poke at snapping turtles, though.

And I remember fishing in a little local stream we called The Brook. God, I remember every detail of the bottom, every twist and turn, how the bottom dropped away where The Brook bent sharply to the right at the foot of a big oak, that the water above a certain log far downstream always—*always*—held two trout that would eat a Muddler Minnow, that the sandbar above the long riffle was a good place to look for turtles. The Brook taught me about trout and moving water. I last fished there about ten years ago, by which time The Brook had become little more than a drainage ditch for a golf course and condo development. I caught one scrawny hatchery rainbow on a gray midge. I killed the fish rather than return it to such water, and then left before any more of my childhood could be taken from me.

Those memories and a thousand more were prompted by the old photos, helped, perhaps, by the good Scotch that accompanied my reminiscences. I don't remember learning to cast or tie knots, nor do I recall lessons in finding or handling fish. Yet I learned all that stuff. Long before I kissed a girl for the first time, I knew how to find a trout, catch it, and clean it. While I was still getting around on a Schwinn three-speed, I knew how to hold a perch or a pickerel, how to mend my fly line so a garden worm would swing into the slack water behind a midstream rock, how to tie a clinch knot that would hold. Years before the scent of perfume meant anything to me, I was intimately familiar with the fertile smell of bluegills bedding in the shallows, and I knew how to make popping bugs that would catch the randy sunfish.

I guess I absorbed fishing gradually over the course of many happy mornings and evenings. I know I was, and am, uncommonly lucky in having a good teacher, a man who was preparing to become an angling mentor even when he posed in front of his father's camera nine years before my birth, and who, half a century later, still loves to talk about fishing and the old days, and still doesn't mind picking out his kid's backlashes.

Dad taught me more than techniques and skills, though he taught those very well. He taught me to appreciate good gear, and especially to appreciate the skillful use of any tackle. He prefers words such as "style" and "class" to terms such as "grace," yet all his fishing, even dunking doughballs for carp or pieces of bread for catfish, is imbued with grace. Dazzling the rubes, as he puts it, is one of the rewards of angling gracefully.

Most important of all, he taught and lives something I can only call the code, a subtle *ethos* far too long and complex ever to be written down. The code includes the big things: respect for the quarry and its habitat, consideration of other sportsmen, patience, a degree of fortitude, and humor in the face of self-inflicted discomfort. In the old, politically incorrect days, much of the code came under the heading of manliness. But it entails other things, too. It involves knowing why sometimes it's good to cast to a bass in the shallows, and why sometimes it's better to hold the cast and just wish the fish luck on its morning hunt. It involves sitting in a canoe, silent and still, watching a heron look for frogs or minnows, and knowing that you're watching the best fishing of the day. It involves laughing as hard as you can when you lip a fat, greedy largemouth and see the tail of a mouse or crayfish sticking out of the fish's craw. Very often, it includes poking at snapping turtles or catching leopard frogs with your hands or marveling at the mating dance of mayflies while trout rise all around you.

To know the code is to be an angler. Not to know it is to be someone who merely tries to hook fish.

I sometimes wonder how people learn to be anglers nowadays. A lot of kids are growing up without fathers around, and no matter how hard you try, you can't replace dads. Paid instructors cannot teach the code. Becoming an angler is not merely a matter of belonging to a certain demographic group, of purchasing the right name-brand equipment, of learning the right buzzwords, or even of mastering a bunch of skills.

I wonder how much of the code I've taught my daughters. They're teenagers now, interested in things other than fishing, and my time for teaching the important stuff has passed. I hope I gave them some of what Dad gave me. We've gone fishing plenty of times, Ellie and Amy and I, and we've caught frogs with our hands and we've poked at turtles and snakes. They've helped me dig worms—when she was little, Amy put the pink worms, which she decided were girls, in one can, and the brown boy worms in another—and they can put their own bait on their hooks. Many years ago, in a remnant of the Morris Canal, Amy caught sixty-four crawdads by carefully, patiently lifting each one from the water after it had seized a bit of worm stuck on a hook. She has the right instincts. The first time she held a bluegill, when she was six years old, it squirmed in her hand and cut her with its dorsal spines, but she didn't cry. Amy was proud that she didn't cry when her fish cut her. I was, too. She might not remember that day, but I do.

I remember the girls' first fish: Amy's was a bullhead; Ellie's was a big crappie. We have a picture of Ellie and the crappie and me. Of the bullhead we have no photo, but Amy and I remember how it latched on to my thumb and wouldn't let go. She laughed for a long time about the fish stuck on my hand.

Both girls, thank God, have been fishing with their grandpa. They caught astonishing numbers of white perch and bluegills off the back of Dad's boat on Greenwood Lake, and they paid attention while my father showed them how to handle and unhook the fish. Later, after my parents retired and moved, the girls caught channel catfish from a dock in Florida while alligators swam within fifty feet of us. They can handle a canoe, they love fast motorboats, and they've a healthy respect for, but no fear of, snakes and snapping turtles.

I've had little time to teach them, particularly in recent years. I work and I worry, and they grow up. Ellie has her own car and a part-time job, and Amy plays field hockey. Too soon, Ellie will have picked a college and Amy will be thinking about her driver's license. Time goes faster and faster, and I grow older, and I worry that the chain that started at my grandfather's cabin on Paulinskill Lake has been broken.

But maybe it hasn't. Fishing has not informed their childhoods the way it informed mine, and I don't think either of them will grow up to be a passionate angler. But perhaps my girls have learned just enough of the magic and wonder of fish and wild places to carry them through life. They both like frogs, and they both know to avoid a bluegill's spines and a bullhead's pectoral fins.

Amy went camping with a friend and her family recently. She asked if she could bring a couple of rods and some lures so she and her friend could fish. Her friend caught a perch that Amy unhooked without getting hurt by its gill flaps. When they snagged lures in trees and broke them off, Amy tied on new lures with good clinch knots.

Last semester, Ellie and a friend did a science-class report on black bears. Every day after school, the girls traipsed around the mountains here in southern Vermont looking for bear sign. Ellie's mom worried, as mothers will, that the girls would find more than sign. But Ellie and her classmate hiked for dozens of miles, compiled tons of data on bears, and always came home safe and sound. They had fun, too.

Maybe I've done okay. I hope to hell I have. The gift I've enjoyed should last longer than I will.

The summer before I turned forty, I made a trip to Florida for the first time in almost two years. My grandfather had taken ill and was in the hospital recuperating from an operation. I went south to see him and lend some moral support to my dad, who had reached the excruciating knowledge that it was time for his father to enter a nursing home.

I was too late: about an hour before I left for the airport, Dad called to say that Pop-Pop had died. I recall a bad, terrifying landing in Orlando, but have no other memory of the flight to Florida. I was thinking about Paulinskill and a few other things.

Dad and I had planned to do a little fishing between trips to the hospital. We had not planned to deal with my grandfather's passing. Some people might not understand, but we went fishing anyway. We had to. I needed to fish with my father, the best angler I will ever see, and I guess he needed to fish with his boy.

We took Dad's new boat to a body of water called Lake Marian. The lake drains into a creek that runs between tall cattails and through swamps and eventually breaks up in the jungle that still covers the parts of central Florida that the Disney Corporation hasn't torn up and paved. We put in when it was barely light, like we used to do in the old days. Mist covered the water and birdsong filled the air. The little Japanese outboard didn't make as much blue smoke as the old Evinrude did, but it made enough to satisfy my nostrils.

Dad steered straight for the creek. In the midsummer heat, of course, it made sense to fish in the creek. But the whereabouts of bass had little to do with why Dad pointed the boat toward Lake Marian's outlet and shoved the throttle all the way forward. We needed to go upstream again, he and I, no matter which way the current was running.

We fished for a while at the mouth of the creek, throwing big buzzbaits with plug-casting outfits and cranking them back. A couple of bait fishermen showed up and set out their lines, so we entered the creek, Dad steering us into the fog.

We cast buzzbaits and plastic worms to the banks for several hours, talking a little about this and that, but mostly justly throwing and cranking. Dad ran the electric motor from his seat near the bow, guiding the narrow boat between the walls of vegetation. We saw herons and egrets and some birds whose names I don't know. At Paulinskill, I remembered, there were birds my grandfather named go-ahead birds because they always went ahead of the boat, jumping up and flying a hundred yards at a time as we moved down the lake or up the stream. I don't know the real names of the go-ahead birds, either, but I don't have to.

As we entered the thick jungle, we saw a baby alligator in front of the boat. Dad cast near it a couple times, and we laughed when the little gator turned toward the sound of his plastic worm hitting the water. Had the gator stayed put, no doubt we would have poked at it with the paddle as we drew abreast of it.

It had been raining a lot in central Florida, the lake was high, and we were able to go farther down the creek than Dad had ever gone before. The creek got narrower and the current got faster, and we kept throwing and cranking as the water pushed us along.

Inevitably, we ran aground. The bottom of the outboard caught in the sand right before the creek entered a genuinely scary swamp, just as we started to wonder aloud if it was time to turn back. We were stuck right and proper, and the outboard motor is hard to raise from inside the boat. For a moment, we thought one of us would have to get out and, if the bottom was solid enough to support a man's weight, tow the boat out of the shallows by the anchor rope, like Humphrey Bogart pulling the *African Queen* through the swamp. But Dad cranked the bow-mounted electric motor up to full power, and very slowly, it pulled the little boat around against the current. I pushed from the stern with the paddle, the outboard came unstuck, and we started to move against the current.

Dad fired up the outboard when we were clear of the shallow water. He shoved the throttle all the way forward and steered us between the tall cattails, keeping the boat in the channel, one hand on the throttle and the other on the tiller. We probably went faster than we should have, but I wasn't worried.

When we got back to the lake, we fished for a while in the late-morning heat. Dad caught a nice bass on a buzzbait, the only fish of the day. I threw and cranked and threw and cranked, my wrist growing tired from the unfamiliar effort of casting with a stout plug rod. But I was content to make so many casts without getting a backlash that Dad had to pick out. It occurred to me that maybe, as I neared forty, I was getting the hang of fishing.

Then Dad asked, "You wanna race around the lake?" and I said yes, and we made the circuit of Lake Marian as fast as the little outboard could push us. We spooked a big, dozing alligator as we roared up on it, and I saw the gator's white belly when it rolled onto one side before diving. I blinked hard and saw painted turtles jumping off logs in Paulinskill Lake when they heard the blue Evinrude approaching. The breeze felt fine, the motor made the good old rattling two-stroke roar, and for a few minutes I was ten years old and my dad was a young man again and the boat went just fast enough to outrun our grief.

In his old age, Norman Maclean wrote of being haunted by waters. When I was younger, I thought I knew what he meant, but I didn't really. A young man cannot be haunted by waters: he wades too confidently and energetically; he is too intent on casting well and hooking fish.

In middle age, feeling my way along a slippery bottom and casting blindly most of the time, I begin to understand what Maclean wrote. I shall not go upstream again in the way I once did. The smell of a pond and the *smack* of a bluegill picking a nymph off the underside of a lily pad make me look back as much as they make me look forward. I know that sometimes I deliberately throw my line into the past.

But always I feel the tug of happy times. Things remind me of boyhood, of adventures no one will ever top, and of days with two men who made me an angler and opened the gate to an entire world.

Haunted by waters? Maybe sometimes, when the breeze is just right or I smell outboard exhaust or the sun glints a particular way off a spiderweb wet with dew.

Mostly, though, I am blessed by waters.

*Vermont, 1997*

## CHAPTER 8

# *Ixnay the Atinlay*

THE TROUT FISHING I LIKE BEST DOESN'T BEGIN UNTIL AFTER THE Fourth of July. Opening Day still brings a twinge of the old urgency, but it passes. Early spring in New England is not a season to be taken seriously, and I'm long past the need to stand in a dirty, thirty-eight-degree stream just because I have not caught a trout in six months.

May brings better water and the Hendricksons, and maybe one or two model days of the dry-fly ritual when I cast flies tied with good hackle and genuine wood-duck fibers to rising trout. It's pleasant fishing in a tweedy, *faux*-British sort of way, but a couple of three-hour stretches of it are enough. I feel pretty much the same way about champagne: the first glass tastes fine, but by the third, no matter how good the vintage, I'm looking for a potted plant where I can dump the stuff. Hell would be an eternity of hatch matching on a river shared with tweedy savants.

Besides, the bass and sunfish start to wake up in May, and I'd rather fish for them. By Memorial Day, the largemouths are chasing little fish and frogs in the shallows, and chasing the bass keeps me happy through June and into July. After Independence Day, the fishing changes. The evening bite diminishes, my topwater lures work less well, and the bass seem to lose the edge of their appetite.

Or maybe I'm the one that changes. After a month of paddling Jitterbugs across the surface and ripping spinnerbaits through foot-deep water, after catching dozens of snotty bass exactly the way I like to catch them, perhaps my appetite for largemouths loses its edge. As the hot weather begins, I can still catch some early in the morning with a Texas-rigged plastic worm or a slow-rolled spinnerbait, but my need to hook a bass has shrunk. I've had the best of the season; it will get me by for a while.

And so it's time to go trout fishing in the little headwater streams. By mid-July, they're low, clear, and empty of other fishermen. The big hatches are done, and that's fine with me. In town, the temperature is over ninety and tourists wilt on the sidewalks, but it's ten degrees cooler under the green canopy that covers the brooks that run icy cold even through August's worst heat wave.

I put on old hip boots and carry a soft, short, fiberglass 4-weight rod I built myself. I usually wear my vest out of habit, but everything I really need could fit in a shirt pocket: some spare 5X tippet, small forceps, and a 35-millimeter film canister containing a half dozen foam-rubber ants, size 14. They are bluegill bugs writ small, and they rarely let me down. When the ants fail, nothing else works, either.

Although it entails no matching of hatches, no complicated rigging and rerigging to dead-drift a nymph at precisely the right depth beneath an indicator, my midsummer trout fishing satisfies me better than any other kind. The low water turns the fish into nervous wrecks that will not tolerate oafish wading. With trees overhead, I have to throw sidearm, keeping the backcast out of the bushes and squirting the presentation cast under a branch, into a pocket between rocks, or next to the seam where a drowned log divides the current. Sometimes I can't see the little black ant as it drifts; I have to guess where it is and strike when a trout breaks the surface, hoping that the fish has snatched my fake bug and not some tiny caddis or midge.

Maybe its simplicity is what makes high-summer trout fishing so enjoyable. It's a chance to buck the system, to blow a Bronx cheer at the techno-anglers. With a cheap, homemade rod, a hook decorated with a hunk of black sponge and a few strands of black rubber, and a brook that contains just enough trout to provide cause for optimism, I have an antidote to the manufactured complexity that has perverted the sport. This is not high-performance, fussy angling, not the sort of fishing that lets a tiresome Latin-babbling expert trot out his erudition and celebrate his masterly skills acquired over decades of intense study and practice. On a little stream full of trout that think ants are yummy, you do not have to analyze a complex mix of hatches to have any chance of success, or execute complicated aerial mends to ensure a drift that avoids even a hint of microdrag, or tie a subtly different fifteen-foot leader for each pool you fish. All you have to do is exercise a little streamcraft and make a decent twenty-foot cast. I don't even know the Latin names of any ants, and I have lots of fun.

Sometimes I have a comrade in the rebellion against neurotic angling and jargon worship. My friend John has edited his share of fly-fishing twaddle. He gave the name Little Shithole to the brook that runs behind the building where we once held jobs with a publisher of fishing magazines, filling pages with the least implausible stuff we could find.

We don't fish the Little Shithole as often as we used to, but we still flog it a couple times a summer. It's a better stream than John's name for it would indicate, cold and reasonably clean, full of bugs and a mixed population of browns and brookies.

The little river doesn't have enough room for two guys to fish at once, so we take turns. We use entirely different flies—John favors hairwing drys, while I pitch a sponge-rubber ant—but since we switch after every fish, we end the day having each caught the same number of trout, thereby putting the lie to the obsessive hatchmatchery printed in magazines. We have accumulated our own statistics to prove that it's all nonsense.

As we work our way up the stream, we keep up a running mockery of the clichés and claptrap of which we've read too much.

"There *oughtta* be a damn trout there," I say as I flip the rubber ant to a good-looking spot for the fifth time. Then I shift into magazine-speak: "It looks just like what the top experts call a prime lie, providing shade, refuge from the current, a steady supply of food, and ready access to the safety of deeper water. And yet my best presentations fail to yield results."

"I think your problem is a failure to recognize the complexities of the situation," John says, falling into the idiom. "What we have here, if my observations are correct, is a classic *masking* hatch. Although the Great Slate-Winged Mahogany Duns seem most numerous, the fish are actually feeding selectively on the much smaller, crippled emerging females of *Paratendinitis effendi*. Might I suggest a size 28 trailing-shuck pattern with one tail broken off and the wings canted to the left?"

"You may, professor, but I'll stick with the ant."

A trout rises and gobbles my foam-rubber fly.

"Ho! A vicious, *slashing* strike!" John cries. By mutual agreement, the first bite of the day is always a vicious, slashing strike.

"My reel howled in protest—"

"—*screamed* in protest—"

"—*screeched* in protest as another trophy squaretail greyhounded across the pool. My rod bucked and quivered in my hand—"

"An image I'd rather not contemplate, thank you."

"—as I struggled to subdue the leviathan of the North Country."

"A tad purple, that."

"Yeah, you're right. Anyway, here he comes." I steer a seven-inch brookie into my left hand, pop the barbless hook out of his yap, and turn him loose.

"Bye-bye, fishy. Next."

We slosh ten yards upstream, and John begins casting a Hair-Wing Coachman to a tricky eddy below a boulder. We've caught fish here before, but never easily. John throws a soft cast and wiggles some extra slack into the line before it drops to the water. The trick extends his drift by a foot, but the cast goes strikeless.

"Baffling," John says. "That fly is a perfect imitation of peacock herl and calf hair on a hook. Even the most educated trout usually can't resist it."

"Microminidrag," I say. "I can spot it from here. The turbulence caused by the vortex of conflicting currents is acting on your leader and making your fly behave unnaturally. These hyperselective wild trout never come up for a less-than-perfect presentation."

"Maybe I should add another nine feet of 10X tippet, as many savvy anglers recommend," John says, flicking another cast to the top of the eddy. The savvy angler is to fishing gazettes what the plucky gal is to sensational tabloid weeklies.

"That would help. But I think the situation's hopeless unless you employ the Austrian Spiral Staircase Cast, which creates eight times as much slack as the distance between you and the fly."

"I was thinking of trying the Triple Murtchison Backhand Mend," John says. "I read about it in a magazine, and it looked like you don't need more than four hands to do it."

He rolls his line into the air and drops the bushy fly into the eddy again. We both see the flash of yellow as a trout, a pretty nice one by Shithole standards, comes up for the fly.

"The wily and elusive brown trout!" I holler. Browns, by definition, are always wily and elusive.

"A sledgehammer strike that nearly tore the rod from my grasp!" John says. "I grudgingly yielded line as the red-spotted brute surged into the fast water, wondering if the gossamer tippet—notice how they're always friggin' gossamer?—would withstand the pressure."

"Want me to throw some water on that reel? Looks like your carbon-fiber and titanium disk drag is starting to smoke."

"That's from my cigarette."

"Oh. Well, keep his head up. Give him the butt."

"I'd rather fight him down and dirty," John says. "What other clichés ya got?"

The trout helps by picking that instant to jump.

"Whoa! The crystalline surface of the stream exploded in a shower of diamonds—"

"Is it crystal or diamond? Don't mix minerals."

"—as the massive brown took to the air in a desperate attempt to throw the hook. And the outdoor writer's handbook doesn't saying anything about not mixing minerals. Looks like a pretty good fish."

"Not bad," John says. He slides a hand under the trout's belly. "About a foot. It just shows the importance of mastering entomology. Your turn. Why don't you see if there's a fish under that bush up yonder?"

My first cast hangs the ant on a branch. I swear and give the line a yank, and the ant pops free, landing about where I wish I'd thrown it in the first place.

"Aha! The *ultra*-natural off-the-bush presentation!" John says. "The ultimate in advanced terrestrial fishing."

"Secrets of the pros, revealed," I add.

So it goes for another hour. We land three trout apiece and make fun of the stuff we've read and perpetrated in magazines, making up bogus Latin names for bugs and inventing techniques that would work only if all of Isaac Newton's work was dead wrong. It's my turn to fish when we reach the spot we call the Paradise Pool, a long, calm, uncommonly pretty stretch of water. The stream opens up here, and though the Paradise Pool rarely yields more than one fish, it looks like it should hold a dozen. You could put a picture of it next to the entry for "trout stream" in the dictionary.

Since we have room to work out some line, we usually fish the Paradise Pool with longer casts. After an hour and a half of the Little

Shithole's close-quarters fishing, it feels good to stretch out a bit. Sometimes we never move out of the foot of the pool and take turns throwing double-hauls to the choppy water at the head sixty feet away.

I make a few token medium-range casts to the middle of the pool, raising one tiddler that misses the ant, and then give in to the fun of slinging a long string. Like a lot of soft, technically inferior rods, my little glass stick will move a fair amount of line if you make its midsection and butt do the work. I can't always reach the head of the pool, but today my stroke is good. The rubbery rod bends all the way down to the cork, grunts, and sends the line on its way with enough zip to deposit the fly better than fifty feet away.

"Wow. Is that one of them ninety-million-modulus IM27 rods I read about?" John asks. "Those new jobs that are lighter yet stronger, so you can cast farther with less effort to make pinpoint presentations with precise imitations of the naturals?"

"Even better than that," I reply. "This one is computer engineered with a variable compound progressive taper that provides the ideal combination of delicacy and power."

"Gee. Does the resin system incorporate a new, proprietary space-age polymer?"

"Damn right. This puppy's made with plastic nearly as advanced as the stuff in a screwdriver handle."

"You *must* be a pro. What's a high-performance rod like that cost?"

"I hate to brag, but I've got about forty-two fifty tied up in this baby," I say, lifting the line to begin another cast. "Of course, that includes a reel seat that has gen-yoo-wine wood."

I heave another ambitious cast to the head of the pool. It's a silly thing to do, of course. No doubt I've lined and spooked at least one trout I could have caught with a shorter cast. If a trout does come up for the fly, he'll have to hook himself, because seven feet of mushy fiberglass is not the tool for setting a hook at long range. But it doesn't matter. I've caught a few fish and I feel like giving the arm some exercise.

A trout rises and eats the fly almost immediately, pulls hard for just a second, and squirts up out of the stream, making one of those high, crazy, end-over-end leaps that one in twenty browns will make. By the time I raise the rod, he has come unstuck. The whole event starts and ends in maybe two heartbeats.

"Perfect," John says. "Classic. Like a magazine cover. Let's get out of here and get some lunch."

As we trudge back to the car, he delivers his usual summary:

"Fish were caught, no one was injured. Latin was uttered only in jest. I pronounce this day a success."

It really is a simple little sport if you want it to be. That's one of the secrets of lucky—and sometimes even savvy—anglers.

*Vermont, 2000*

CHAPTER 9

# *Casting Blindly*

I WENT THROUGH A BRIEF CASE OF PURITY IN MY EARLY THIRTIES, forsaking all other tackle in favor of the fly rod. It happens to a lot of anglers, and some never recover.

During my purist spell, I heard about a place called the Trophy Stretch, a special-regulations section of a river I'd never fished. Several of my acquaintances seemed to regard the Trophy Stretch as a promised land, though none of them had anything definite to say about it. Big trout, they'd heard, though none of them had actually seen the great beasts. Hatches, they added, though none could say precisely of what. Fly fishing only, they pointed out. A refuge from the barbarian hordes. My acquaintances at the time, suburbanites like me, seemed in love with the idea of the place.

I looked up the river in the fishing-regulations booklet and found it on a map. It was about an hour from home, and it was indeed a fly-fishing-only piece of water. The "trophy" designation, I guessed, derived from proximity to the state's biggest hatchery and its tanks full of breeders. No matter. The main thing was that I'd found some new water, a stretch of river protected by special regulations and frequented by kindred spirits. It needed investigating.

So Mary Jo and I deposited the girls at Grandma's house on a Friday night in June, got up before the sun on Saturday, and made the drive to the Trophy Stretch. Predictably, it was a disappointment, a drab little river flowing sluggishly through an endless tangle of underbrush. Without the big breeders dumped in by the hatchery guys, it would have been just another creek-chub brook, and not a very attractive one. The promised land, in my experience, rarely lives up to the promise.

But though we caught nothing in the Trophy Stretch, our morning there was not without enlightenment. On the path between the parking area and the river, we ran into a fellow angler, a young guy decked out in expensive waders and name-brand vest. We stopped to exchange pleasantries. He asked if we'd fished the Trophy Stretch before, and I told him no, hoping he'd volunteer some advice.

Instead of suggesting a place to start, he asked where I usually fished.

I named my home stream, a sorely abused river I'd lived near for most of my life.

"Jesus Christ," our brother of the angle spat. "How the hell can you stand to fish with all those goddamn *spin fishermen?* Goddamn slobs oughtta be outlawed. Christ, I'd rather not fish than put up with those friggin' spin fishermen."

He said "spin fishermen" the way a redneck preacher might say "devil worshipper" or "sodomite." It was impressive to hear so much vitriol packed into four syllables. I've heard decent folk speak of child molesters and godless communists with less contempt and loathing.

Then, having condemned everyone not exactly like him, he tromped off.

The encounter took some of the bloom off the morning and might help explain why we fished with less than our usual gleeful enthusiasm. But it started me thinking, and it might have been the first step in my recovery from purity.

A decade and a half later, I still remember that silly bastard's tackle. His nymph-fishing rig had a hefty split shot on the tippet and a huge orange bobber (sorry—strike indicator) on the leader butt. That's an efficient setup for hooking trout, but for grace, pleasure, and sport, it ranks well below cane-poling for crappies with live minnows.

And yet the guy wielding it couldn't stand to be around spin fishermen. He was a *fly* fisher, and therefore better.

It is, alas, a common attitude. Naturally, every variety of angler thinks that his version of sport is best. The spinnerbait expert believes that the plastic-worm fanatic wastes a lot of his time. The big-game saltwater angler will not trifle with piddling bass and pike. The ultra-light enthusiast feels sorry for anglers who miss all the fun by fishing with heavy line and robust rods. The accomplished bait fisherman wonders why other guys bother with inherently inferior methods.

But none of them hates, loathes, despises, ridicules, libels, and slanders people who fish differently. That mindset belongs to fly-fishing purists.

A famous fly fisher of my acquaintance refers to spin fishermen as "zip gunners." Other purists prefer the terms "yahoos" and "bubbas" for folks who use spinning or casting tackle. "Unwashed masses" also comes up in conversations among fly rodders.

While chatting with a friend at a fly-fishing show some years ago, I allowed "spinnerbait" to escape my lips.

"Hey—quit swearing," a man in the crowd said.

"Huh? Me?"

"Yeah. You said 'spinner,'" the man replied. "That's a swear word as far as I'm concerned. Goddamn things oughtta be outlawed."

The source of this piscatorial bigotry is a mystery. I suspect that some of it might stem from an ego-boosting syllogism that runs something like this:

> *Fly fishing requires extraordinary intelligence, perception, and nobility of character. Anyone who fly-fishes possesses these attributes.*
> *I fly-fish.*
> *Therefore, I possess extraordinary intelligence, perception, and nobility of character.*

That's an easy fallacy to fall into. After all, the fly-fishing magazines spout it in every issue. As well they should: it's good business. In the real world, though, you can't derive valid conclusions from false premises.

Or maybe the snootiness of fly fishers can be explained by a theory espoused by one of my literature professors. This gent argued that upon reaching a certain level of affluence or sophistication (the latter is generally imaginary), most Americans begin secretly to wish that they were Englishmen. He meant that upper-crust Americans yearn for an entrenched class system. Such a yearning seems common among fly fishers.

Don't get me wrong. I'm an unabashed elitist. Put three drinks inside me and I'll start trying to explain why universal, unqualified suffrage is a stupid idea and a lousy foundation for a society. Vermont's annual town meetings, those models of perfect, direct democracy, pretty much sold me on the benefits of a hereditary aristocracy. And I wouldn't belong to any club that would have me as a member.

On the other hand, my upbringing drummed into me a belief in meritocracy. If you're going to proclaim yourself a member of an elite, you'd better be able to justify it.

Snobbish fly fishers try hard to justify their elitism, but they lack evidence. The claim of superior sportsmanship stopped working long ago. These days, a guy catching trout with a super-high-modulus graphite fly rod, a 6X tippet that has a nearly 4-pound breaking strength, and a bar-stock reel with a disk drag has no business lording it over a bloke who uses an ultralight spinning rig with 2-pound-test line and a reel with a drag washer the size of a dime. Quite a few smallmouth-bass fly fishers who favor heavily weighted streamers and bucktails cast them with rods and leaders that can whup the average redfish or striper. They'd raise the challenge by switching to light spinning outfits and little eighth-ounce twister-tail jigs. One famous fly fisher told me about using a tarpon rod and line to throw big poppers at largemouth bass. Even a more typical largemouth-bass outfit—a 9-weight, say—is still way more gun than you usually need for the game. Fly rodders after bonefish typically use 10-pound tippets, yet a lot of the bubbas tossing live shrimp employ soft spinning rods and 6-pound line. Along the Texas coast, artful plug casters catch big seatrout with limber rods and light line—lighter line, in many cases, than their fly-fishing brethren use for tippets.

If sport lies in giving the quarry a chance to get away, then fly fishers are only rarely more sporting than other fisherfolk. Besides, sportsmanship does not reside in the tackle, but in the hands that wield it. Or, to look at it differently, an adept angler can bring sportsmanship to his gear, but the gear cannot confer it on him.

Well, the purist says, that still leaves the question of skill. It takes more than a teaspoon of brains to work a fly rod. Fly fishing, the purist notes, involves the mastery of more and more difficult techniques than any other branch of angling. Editors of fly-fishing magazines have said so.

Of course they have. It's their job. And they're full of baloney.

To fish well with *any* sort of tackle isn't easy. Fly fishers who haven't picked up a spinning rod in thirty years or, worse yet, have never used any other type of tackle shouldn't disparage other methods until after they've mastered them.

And I do mean mastered them. Irrespective of their gear, most anglers never get very good. But the guy who demonstrates a masterly touch with a light spinning rod or a level-wind reel concedes nothing to the best fly fisher.

In the late 1980s, as I was going through my purist spell, my dad suffered a heart attack that nearly killed him. A few weeks after he came home, I drove up to my parents' home to see how he was getting on. I found him sitting in a lawn chair at the edge of the driveway, practicing his plug casting to keep from going stir crazy. He'd set a bucket—just a regular, wash-the-car bucket—at the foot of the double pine tree on the lawn, about seventy feet from the chair.

I stood and watched as Dad threw cast after cast across the lawn, dropping the hard-rubber practice plug into the bucket about nine out of ten times.

"Go stand on the lawn," he said, "between me and the bucket."

I did, and then Dad started throwing sidearm casts, lofting the plug out to his right side and thumbing the spool of the little Shimano reel to steer the three-eighths-ounce chunk of hard rubber *around* me to drop in the bucket. He grinned as he did it, and I began to know that he'd be all right.

If you're good, you're good, and you got that way through practice. The equipment doesn't matter.

Fly fishers who sneer at other types of angling should give some of that plebeian gear a try. Try sidearming a tiny spoon to a foot-wide pocket behind a rock fifty feet across a stream. Try flipping a half-ounce jig into a coffee-can-wide hole in the hydrilla twenty feet away, and then see if you can do it twenty times in a row in a stiff wind. Learn how a level-wind reel will punish you by backlashing all the way down to the arbor when you fail to thumb the spool properly. Play a good trout on a featherweight spinning outfit, backwinding to give the fish line because you can't trust the crude, tiny drag. Learn the subtlety of crawling a plastic worm across the bottom, feeling for the gentle bump that is a bass picking up the worm and not another rock, stick, or lily-pad stalk. Fish with spinnerbaits until you can look at a box full of them and know which combination of blades will appeal to lethargic bass holding in five feet of fifty-six-degree murky water. Shove your thumb into a big, unhappy bass that has a crankbait with six hooks crosswise in its yap, and wonder if you're about to give the fish a chance to get even.

Do all those things, do them well and repeatedly, and then try to keep a straight face while saying that possessing a fly rod makes you an inherently more skillful angler.

I'm sorry, kids, but fly fishing isn't automatically, inherently, universally, infallibly superior, and casting a size 14 Adams doesn't make you spiritually and intellectually better than the guy tossing a little Panther Martin spinner or throwing a big Jitterbug or even soaking a live shiner. Skill merits respect regardless of the equipment, and an oaf is still an oaf no matter how many thousands of dollars' worth of toys he lugs to the water.

There's only one good reason to fish with a fly rod, and that's because you just plain enjoy it. Wielding one does not put you on the fast track to Heaven, so stop trying to sell the world on that notion. We heathens find it tiresome.

Cast a fly because it feels good, because it gives you pleasure and satisfaction, because, whether or not it's better, it's not like anything else. And because sometimes it's the best way to catch fish. Those reasons are plenty good enough. Let's stop manufacturing class systems to justify our personal brands of fun.

Besides, once you lighten up, you might find that it's fun to use other kinds of tackle, too. Maybe you'll discover that a smallmouth feels pretty good on a light spinning rod, or that it's deeply satisfying to make long, accurate casts with a level-wind reel, riding the spool with feather-light pressure of your thumb to drop the plug into a gap in the lily pads. Maybe you'll even learn that there's something to be said for impaling a big shiner on a hook and watching a float while you wait for a pickerel to show up.

I believe it was the immortal Commander Cody and the Lost Planet Airmen who said it in a song: "I ain't never had *too* much fun."

New tackle shops attract me the way a low-speed car wreck at an intersection draws lawyers, and when one opened in our town, I soon paid it a visit. It was a swank little joint with racks full of expensive fly rods and glass cases housing equally costly reels. Boxes containing $50 fly lines hung on pegs behind the counter. No bait tanks, no buzzbaits, no zipper-lock bags full of squishy plastic worms.

Packages of fly-tying materials covered one wall. A fancy fly-tying desk occupied the corner, and behind the desk sat a pale, morbidly obese man slowly constructing an elaborate fancy-dress salmon fly out of an array of expensive, exotic materials, a fly that would never get wet because it was destined for a shadowbox. A classic, as the salmon-fly tiers like to call them, even when they make up the whole pattern from scratch.

I needed some tying stuff—chenille or black rabbit strips or something—so I moseyed over to the materials display. The fat man took his eyes off his creation and looked me up and down.

He asked if I was a fisherman. Odd question, considering the context. I replied that indeed I am.

"Been out lately?" he asked as he poked around on the desk for a feather plucked from the skin of what had been the last living specimen of some tropical bird.

I told him that a friend and I had been up to the reservoir over the mountain a few days earlier, and that we'd caught a few smallmouths.

"Smallmouths? Bass?" he said. He monkeyed around with the feather for moment, then looked up again. "Well, that's *okay.* You know, there's nothing *wrong* with a little bass fishing." He sounded like a priest giving absolution to a penitent, or some new-age counselor excusing a particularly deviant practice. "In fact, it's kind of nice to pull a no-brainer every now and then, isn't it? Makes you appreciate the *real* fishing."

I didn't know what to say. This lard-ass clown looked like he hadn't been outdoors in a decade, and here he was casually insulting me, my fishing, and the bass.

Then he asked if I knew anything about fly tying and began to blither about his fancy salmon fly and the great skill, indeed the genuine artistic genius, that it takes to assemble such things.

I told him no, I didn't tie flies, and got out of the joint pronto without buying anything. I can't stand to be around people like that.

*South Carolina, 2002*

CHAPTER 10

# *A Beatific Vision*

BACK WHEN THE INDIANS OWNED THE NEIGHBORHOOD, THE LITTLE stream had probably been clear and icy cold. No doubt it once held brook trout. It took its first hit in the mid–1700s, when English settlers began turning the forest into hardscrabble farms. Towns sprouted on the new landscape, and a few rugged entrepreneurs built mills powered by the brook, throwing small dams across the water wherever there seemed to be a good spot. After the Civil War, other, wealthier entrepreneurs built a railroad up the valley so that Vermont's timber, produce, wool, and dairy products could reach markets to the south. In places, the tracks paralleled the course of the brook. The towns grew. The last of the old-growth trees became furniture, paper, or firewood. Photos taken in the 1890s show a countryside almost devoid of trees. By the middle of the twentieth century, the little stream probably bore scant resemblance to its former self. I'd guess that it held few brook trout by then.

In the late 1970s, someone decided that the stream needed a bigger dam that would turn part of it into a small lake. The dam got built, the water backed up, and the state stocked the new lake with bass, crappies, yellow perch, bluegills, pumpkinseeds, and bullhead catfish. Fifteen years later, when I first saw the place, the lake had become a passable warm-water fishery.

Fanatical purists might regard that as a sad story, another example of a once-pristine trout stream degraded to the level of bluegill water. I, a heathen, was grateful for the variety that the man-made lake provided. Maybe some guys can live by trout alone, but I can't, and I was happy that someone had decided to swap three-quarters of a mile of slow, moribund, doomed brook for forty acres of bass and crappie fishing.

The old railroad tracks, hardly ever used nowadays, run past the dirt parking lot and over a bridge that crosses the dam's spillway. On early summer evenings, I'd string up a light fly rod or a medium plug-casting outfit, walk across the bridge, and fish the riprap along the dam face or the weed beds along the far shore. The locals who wanted to fill coolers with triple limits of stocked trout tended to stick close to the parking lot, and many evenings I had the riprap and weeds to myself as I cast for sunfish, crappies, and largemouths. Once or twice a summer, a friend and I would take a canoe out onto the lake and explore the upstream end. We rarely caught anything note-worthy up in the creek, but we'd see beavers and muskrats and big snapping turtles, and that was enough to make the paddling worth-while.

The old tracks ran the other way, of course, into the woods beyond the parking lot. For several years, I wondered if they'd provide access to any good bank-fishing spots near the head of the lake or even up on the creek. Late one fall, after an hour of fruitless fishing, I decided to follow the tracks and find out. I stowed my rod in the car and fol-lowed the rail bed into the woods.

The tracks curved for a few hundred yards and then straightened. I knew that the lake's shoreline bent around in the same direction, so I was still hopeful that the tracks would eventually lead me to water.

Sure enough, they did. After maybe half a mile, I could see water through the brush on my left. A few paths led down to fishing spots on the bank. I could tell they were fishing spots by the profusion of empty bait containers and hook packages lying on the ground amid tangles of monofilament. Had these been places where feral teenagers gathered at night, they would have been marked by broken beer bottles, used condoms, and a pair or two of panties decorating the shrubbery. Outdoor editors learn to distinguish subtle indications.

I pressed on, deeper into the woods, and found a wondrous thing. Up where the creek enters the lake, on the other side of the railroad tracks and invisible to anyone fishing the lake from a canoe, I found a long, skinny pond. The near end was marshy, full of cattails and grass. But as I walked along the tracks, I could see that the bottom fell away and the narrow pond quickly became very deep. I couldn't see the bottom, even though the water had only the slightest tinge of green. Old, waterlogged timber littered the edges of the water. A thick patch of lily pads floated next to the rocky point on the far bank, just within range of a good cast with a plug rod. A tangle of drowned trees filled the shallow water at the far end of the pond.

It was easy to see what had happened. When the railroad came through four or five or six generations ago, the guys building it had run into a long stretch of swampy ground along the brook. So they'd dug up tons and tons of dirt and rocks to make what amounted to a causeway for the rail bed, creating a long, deep borrow pit in the process. Many years later, other guys decided to turn part of the stream into a lake. As the water rose, some seeped through the old causeway, filling the borrow pit and turning it into a pond with the same level as the lake. That's my guess, anyway.

No matter how it got there, it was new water, and very good-looking water. Several paths ran down the steep embankment to small level spots on the water's edge. I inched down each path, placing my feet carefully. Along the embankment, the pond's bottom dropped away at about a sixty-degree angle. A misstep would mean going for a swim.

The place obviously got some attention from fishermen—the forked sticks and empty worm containers said so—but it seemed less frequently used than the bankside spots on the lake. As I explored the shoreline, I saw a few bluegills and small bass. Baby sunfish and bass flitted around at the edge of the water. An immense snapping turtle, a beast with a shell that would have covered a garbage-can lid, surfaced in the middle of the pond. Things were getting interesting.

Deep water, rocks, a hard bottom, piles of drowned timber, lily pads and other vegetation, marshy areas that would harbor frogs and minnows, overhanging trees, bass, sunfish, evidence of propagation, and little evidence of serious fishing pressure—the new pond qualified as a find that merited diligent investigation. I made a mental note never to leave my rod in the car when I went exploring.

I was standing on the tracks and contemplating going back for my tackle when I heard the drumming of hooves around the next bend. The noise came closer, and I eased off the side of the tracks, onto the brushy ground that led down to the creek. If someone was running a horse along the rail bed, I didn't want to be in the way.

Then a deer, a huge, fat doe, came around the bend running hell-bent-for-election down the tracks. There was nothing chasing her, so I stepped onto the tracks and jumped up and down, waving my arms. She skidded to a stop fifty yards away, nearly going ass over teakettle on the railroad ties, eyeballed me for two seconds, then spun around and sprinted back the way she'd come, her white flag pointing skyward. I decided that I, too, should retrace my steps, and I ambled back to the car.

If the weather holds, I told myself, I'll try the pond tomorrow or the day after. The tail end of October is no time to be bass fishing in Vermont, but you never know.

The weather didn't hold, of course. We had several days of cold rain and high winds, and suddenly Indian summer turned into winter. In New England, you can sometimes feel the season change; it happens that quickly. It's not so much a question of temperature as of the quality of the light, or maybe the mood of the woods and sky and water. You step outside and just know that autumn is over or summer has begun.

The new pond would have to wait until spring. I thought about it a lot during the winter. It had to hold some good bass—just had to. Fly fishing was out of the question: no room anywhere to use the long rod. Crankbaits would hang up instantly on all those old, drowned trees. A Texas-rigged plastic worm might be useful in spots. A spinnerbait seemed the best way to prospect the pond, at least until things warmed up enough for me to start throwing topwater plugs or buzzbaits in the evenings. Or would mornings be better? Would the big fish stay mostly in the deep water, or would they eat frogs and small rodents in the shallow ends of the pond early and late in the day? I thought about the pond a lot during the months when icicles grow from the eaves.

I had a frantic spring full of magazine deadlines and crises and cool, wet weather. It was almost June when I went back to the pond, armed with a stout casting rod and an assortment of spinnerbaits and plugs. I wondered if I'd have to share the place with yahoos who drop their bait containers and hook packages and beer bottles on the ground.

The yahoos must still have been busy with hatchery trout, and I had the pond to myself. I stood on the tracks at the marshy end for twenty minutes, savoring the late-May smell of things turning green and listening to frogs and watching the water. A few fish made small dimples or ripples or bulges. The big snapper poked his head out of the water. Mosquitoes and black flies hummed around my head, looking for a patch of skin not slathered with bug dope. The light had a faint golden tint. I knew that we'd have a few more chilly nights, but summer had come.

I had no clue what to cast, so I tied on one of the old reliables, a white and chartreuse, quarter-ounce spinnerbait with a single, size 4 Colorado blade. You can slow-roll such a lure, crank it through the mid-depths, pump it along the tops of sunken wood, burn it on the surface, or just let it flutter down at the edge of a weed bed or drop-off. Fly-fishing purists don't like to hear it, but their art pales in comparison to the subtleties and versatility of the spinnerbait.

The first path down to the water looked like a death trap, or at least a chute that would project me into six feet of water if I slipped on one of the loose rocks. Twenty yards along the tracks, the second path seemed less hazardous. I shuffled crab-style down to the water's edge, my knees bent and my arms held out for balance, and found a perch where I just had room to swing the plug rod.

I set my tackle bag on a flat rock, checked my drag, and thumbed the reel into freespool. Then, even as my wrist cocked for the cast, I caught something in the corner of my vision, glanced down and to my left, and saw Her.

She was suspended just above the bottom in about three feet of water, hovering over one of the few level spots, about six feet off the bank and maybe ten feet from me. I watched her gills working and her pectoral fins waving slowly back and forth. She turned a little, very slowly, and looked at me. Looked me right in the eye. No fear. None at all. Curiosity, maybe. Contempt, almost certainly.

*Well,* the eyes said, *what the hell do you think you're up to?*

I stood there, not breathing, my arm frozen partway through a cast. I have seen eight-pound largemouth bass in Florida, and She was much bigger. She did not have the bloated girth typical of bass down south, but She was still a buxom gal, clearly an accomplished trencherwoman, one who sucks in a couple of adult bullfrogs when she feels like a snack.

*Guess you weren't expecting me,* the eyes said. I think She sneered, but maybe it was just the natural curve of her lips.

Length? It's hard to say. Fish always look bigger until you catch them. But I've looked at enough fish to say that had She been a striped bass in the ocean, She would have been a keeper. I have never seen another largemouth bass that matched her length.

She hung in the clear water, the end of her huge tail slowly rippling.

*Didn't bring nearly enough gun, did you?* the eyes said.

Weight? Certainly a state record, and by a good margin. Let's be conservative and put it down as somewhere in the neighborhood of thirteen or fourteen pounds. If She'd had the rounded figure of one of her southern cousins, She'd have been an eighteen-pound fish.

We looked at each other.

*You can't be serious,* the eyes said. *You're out of your league. I have made better men than you sell their tackle and take up golf.*

Slowly, I lowered my casting arm. She backed up a little, but still showed no fear.

*Go ahead if you think you're up to it,* the eyes said. *But are you sure you want a piece of me? Do you feel lucky today, punk?*

I knew I didn't have a chance. She'd made me before I'd even reached the edge of the water. She'd probably forgotten more about lures and baits than I'll ever know.

But an angler has to cast. It's like when a pretty woman sits down two barstools away from a single guy. He has to smile and say hello. Or he'll always wonder.

So I rolled the rod tip in a little circle and tossed the spinnerbait fifteen feet past her. She barely moved her eyes as the lure swam by.

*Pitiful,* the eyes said. Then she turned with matronly dignity and sank into the deep water.

"Jesus Christ," I said. Blasphemy seemed the only appropriate comment.

I looked down the shoreline and saw several of her somewhat smaller sisters hovering at ten-foot intervals a couple yards off the bank. Plump five- and six-pound bass they were, big old girls hanging out in the shallows, fluttering their skirts and waiting for boyfriends to come and dig nests on the bottom.

I threw a long cast down the shoreline and cranked the spinnerbait quickly. One of the big old sows flashed on the lure, but didn't take it. On the next cast, the ladies merely got out of the way of the strange contraption rumbling down their street. A couple of them sank into the deep water.

Eventually, I caught one of the boyfriends. He jumped twice and put up a good fight, but a foot-long male largemouth seemed downright puny after my beatific vision. I went home wondering about her, wondering where I could catch a few eight-inch shiners with which to tempt her, wondering if I should respool the Ambassadeur reel with heavier line, wondering if I'd fish anywhere else that year.

I never caught her, of course. Actually, I didn't try all that hard. And even though I knew where the state-record largemouth lived, I also fished in all my usual places for trout and panfish and run-of-the-mill bass.

By telephone, I told a few friends—guys who live in other states and could never find the pond—about my beatific vision. Most, naturally, had advice on how to catch her. Ten-inch plastic worm, said one. Another recommended fishing a huge spinnerbait early in the morning, or maybe throwing the biggest, muskie-size Jitterbug at night. A third advised that my only hope was to get some *very* big shiners.

One friend said, "Jesus, that's exciting—just to *see* a bass like that. A mother of nations. Did she stick around so you could get a good look at her? Doesn't it make you wonder how *old* a fish like that is? How has she lived so long? And what *else* is in that pond that you don't know about? And in *every* pond?" He prattled on, delighted by my discovery and good luck, never once asking how (or even if) I

intended to catch my huge bass, never suggesting a strategy or recommending a lure.

His, I'd already realized, is the best attitude, or at least the one I
share. I did go back to the long, narrow pond in the woods, and I
did heave all sorts of hardware into the water, and I did catch some
respectable bass. But I never again saw the big old gal, the mother of
nations.

It doesn't matter. Someday, if my casting arm holds out, I will
catch an immense bass. I know that with religious certainty. But I
didn't need to catch *that* immense bass. It was, and is, enough to have
seen her, to know that an artificial, accidental pond that barely covers
two acres can hold such a fish. She shocked and amazed me, gave me
back a sense of wonder at the things waiting to be discovered ten
minutes from home or office. And she gave me encouragement, food
for my imagination, because other little-known, unheralded, thor-
oughly unglamorous waters must hold others like her.

That's a lot for one bass to give, and I do not fret over not having
caught her.

But the next state-record bass I run into had better watch out. A
fisherman can wax philosophical for only so long. And I have
respooled with heavier line.

*South Carolina, 2002*

## CHAPTER 11

# Modern Structure Fishing: A How-to Article

"SEE IT? THAT BIG DARK SPOT?" MY FRIEND EARL ASKED, POINTING to a gap in the weed bed in the middle of the river.

"Yeah, I see it. Looks like the hood from a car."

"You got it. Sixty-nine Electra deuce and a quarter. Real American iron. In its day, the preferred ride of all your classier pimps. They don't build 'em like that anymore. Bet that baby had the four-fifty-five engine. And *real* whitewalls."

Marvelous, I thought. I'm standing in a river listening to a chowderhead reminisce about cars.

"Okay, it's the hood of a *great* car," I said. "What am I supposed to do about it? Go find the rest so you can be a pimp?"

"It *was* the hood of a great car," Earl explained. "Now it's structure. See how it's surrounded by weeds? What you wanna do is drop that little crankbait about six feet above that Buick hood. Crank real slow, just fast enough to keep the line tight. When your lure reaches the upstream end of that hood, crank like a son of a bitch—*rip* that plug across the hood."

"What happens then?"

"Just do it," he said. "You'll find out."

I tossed the quarter-ounce, shallow-running crankbait at the spot Earl had indicated, thumbing the lure down almost exactly six feet above the big hunk of rusty metal. As the little plug reached the upstream end of the hood, I began cranking fast. The lure darted a foot below the surface, wobbling violently as it swept across the bare expanse of the old Buick bonnet.

It never reached the near side of the hood. An eighteen-inch smallmouth shot out of the weeds and clobbered the crankbait, bending my light plug rod nearly to the butt. The fish jumped once, and then tried to bore down into the weeds as I held the rod high and put on all the pressure I dared.

"Keep him out of the weeds!" Earl hollered. "And don't let him drag the line across one of those hinge struts!"

Two minutes later, I reached down and lipped a fat, healthy bass. We admired him for a moment and set him loose. Then I turned to Earl.

"Do you mean you *knew* that there'd be a bass there?" I asked.

"Always is. At least one. That's one of my most reliable spots in the river. Any time you see a hood—or a door or a trunk lid—in the middle of a whole bunch of weeds, that's a spot you wanna fish real carefully."

As he explained why, I began to understand why Earl Morley is the top-rated smallmouth guide on New Jersey's Squillhonnack River. After he'd coached me through a dozen more spots that held big bronzebacks, I began to understand some things I've always done instinctively, but without much conscious thought. And I began to appreciate just how woefully misinformed most anglers are when it comes to structure fishing.

Over the next year, I fished with and interviewed a number of highly respected guides on rivers and lakes all across the country. All of them are specialists in what Gil Sanchez of South Wollabar, Indiana, calls "real-world structure." To a man, they agree that fishing magazines and books have been steering fishermen down the wrong path.

All savvy anglers understand the importance of "structure," that catch-all term for any change in the contour, shape, or composition of the bottom, and for objects near which fish will hold. We all know to look for bass where a gravel bar drops off into deeper water, or where a submerged point in a reservoir meets a lush bed of coon-tail weeds. None of us will pass up a stand of drowned timber. Fish like such places; they relate to changes in the bottom, edges, and objects.

By and large, though, fishing authors have ignored the far larger class of objects most anglers see (yet overlook) where they fish. Maybe, as some of my guide friends suggest, the guys who write books and articles want to keep the good stuff for themselves. It seems more likely that most fishing writers are simply out of touch with the real world. After all, they get to take lots of free trips to fancy lodges way out in the boonies, where they fish in pristine waters and have the services of local guides. Most anglers, however, live and fish near population centers. The lessons of Shangri-la do not apply in Shitsville, as my buddy Earl likes to point out.

Fortunately, the experts on real-world structure are happy to share their wisdom, and every angler who lives in the real world can benefit from their lessons.

## TIRES AND RIMS

"You'd figure a tire would serve pretty much the same purpose as a rock, but it doesn't," notes Gil Sanchez. He guides smallmouth anglers on several rivers in northern Indiana, including the Little Kreplak, and has made a study of how discarded tires and wheels attract game fish.

"You see, a rock just kind of sits there in the river," Sanchez says. "Sure, it breaks the current and gives the fish some structure they can relate to, but a tire is better. A tire has a big hole in the middle. Over time, that hole fills with silt, and weeds take root. Now you have a current break, just like a rock, but with built-in vegetation that holds aquatic bugs and stuff. It's almost like a miniature reef system." Several tires are better than one, he notes, but only if they're spread out, not piled atop one another.

Bill Withers of Sandhoonie, Pennsylvania, agrees. "Show me four weed-filled tires flat on the bottom of Waxapoplectic Creek," the noted fly-fishing guide says, "and I'll show you at least a couple of trophy browns." Spring-fed Waxapoplectic Creek flows past a huge auto junkyard that has contributed tons of what Withers calls "steel-belted structure" to the stream.

"Upstream, above the junkyard, you're lucky to catch three trout all day," he points out. "These fish aren't dumb. A bunch of tires—especially the heavier, low-profile radials—stabilizes the riverbed, gives the fish some relief from the current, and once it sprouts some weeds, provides a steady supply of nymphs and scuds. It's perfect habitat."

Withers also likes old rims, with or without tires on them. Nymphs and crayfish crawl through the lug holes and ventilation slots, hiding during the day and coming out at night to forage. A couple of rims on a riverbed should top your list of evening hot spots, Withers advises.

A stretch of river just downstream of a bridge or near a wrecking yard is an obvious place to look for tire structure, but don't confine your fishing to these areas. Experts point out that tires, even those on rims, can travel pretty far downstream from their entry points, particularly during high water.

"That's the great thing about tires," notes Gil Sanchez. "You can find them way back in the woods, a mile from the nearest road or junkyard. You can get away from the more crowded places and still find excellent structure while enjoying a wilderness experience."

## ENGINES

An afternoon with Squint McGonigle teaches you the subtleties of internal-combustion engines. A smallmouth guide on West Virginia's

Blacklung River, Squint has some strong opinions on engines as structure.

"A complete engine with the head and manifolds and oil pan ain't much good," he told me as we drifted downstream in his camo-pattern canoe. "There ain't no place for crawfish or minows or bugs to hide in an engine like that. It might as well just be a big old rock."

But a short block stripped of the cylinder head, oil pan, and ideally, timing-chain cover is a different story, he says. "If the lifter galleys and water jackets are exposed, and if that crankcase is wide open, then all sorts of critters will move in, once most of the oil sludge and antifreeze washes out. That short block becomes a regular apartment house for fish food. If the crank and pistons are gone, too, you got yourself a prime piece of structure."

Squint backs up his words with actions. Twice that day, he anchored above stripped V-8 blocks submerged in four feet of water and told me to swing my weighted streamer past the old engines. I took three good smallmouths off one block; the other yielded four chunky bass.

That experience clarified something I'd never been able to explain. A trout stream I've fished for years contains two engines in virtually identical pools under bridges. I've made countless casts near the Pinto mill in the pool farther downstream, and though the spot has produced a few trout, it has never fished as good as it looks. In the upstream pool, where an old Chevy straight six rests on the bottom, I nearly always hook a brace of trout.

My afternoon with Squint taught me why: the Chevy block lacks its oil pan and manifolds, giving invertebrates plenty of hidey-holes, while the Pinto engine is virtually complete, with even the carburetor and oil-filler cap in place. It's something to keep in mind as you study the structure in your home waters.

The drawback of most auto and truck engines, of course, is their weight. You won't find many cast-iron blocks very far from bridges or roadside pull-offs along a river. And because most engines are in accessible spots, you might not have this prime structure to yourself.

But Squint is hopeful. Nowadays, he notes, many cars have aluminum engine blocks and cylinder heads. Some of these engines, particularly if they're stripped, are light enough to be lugged quite a distance before disposal. A few of the imports, he told me with a grin, are well within the payload of his canoe, even with two men aboard. The fishing on the Blacklung should keep getting better.

## TRUNKS, HOODS, AND DOORS

"Negative structure" is the term Earl Morley applies to automobile hoods and doors lying on a riverbed. What he means is that an expanse of sheet metal creates a bare spot where weeds can't grow. Anything crossing that open area becomes an easy target for predators.

"In the weeds, a minnow or crawdad can find plenty of places to hide," Earl explains. "But when that sucker crosses a car hood lying on the bottom, he's completely exposed. Smallmouths and trout know that, and they hang around the edges of hoods and trunks, waiting for prey to make a mistake. Then it's *pow*—easy lunch for the fish. That's why that big old Buick Electra hood is such a prime piece of structure—it's more than twenty square feet of open territory. Sometimes I'll find six bass working that same hunk of metal."

Earl is quick to note that not all auto-body parts are equally productive. For one thing, color matters.

"A white hood or trunk isn't much good," he says. "Fish just don't feel comfortable exposing themselves against a white background. Black and dark green are best, though deep blue is always worth a few casts."

Although they create smaller areas of negative structure on the bottom, car doors are nonetheless high on Earl's list of hot spots. Whereas a hood or trunk is only two-dimensional, a door is a three-dimensional structure.

"Doors are thick," he points out, "and they're mostly hollow inside. Lots of crawdads and insects live inside a door, crawling around on the window mechanism and lock and stuff, but when they come out, they're completely exposed for a minute. That's when they get eaten. Whenever you spot a dark door on the bottom, expecially if the window is still in one piece and rolled up, you want to work that spot. Just be careful about getting snagged on a handle or window crank."

## APPLIANCES

Most of the experts I interviewed agree that discarded washing machines, ovens, refrigerators, and the like could be superb structure but for a common drawback: color. "Nine out of ten fridges you find in a river or lake are white," laments Ben Kilgore, who guides anglers on Wyoming's famous Chickenhawk River. "And white just isn't a very good color for structure. Even a cutthroat trout ain't dumb enough to spend much time against a background like that." But he adds that a white appliance in the middle of a thick weed bed merits a few casts. Trout hide in the weeds and then dart out to pick off careless prey silhouetted against the white washer or fridge.

Cletis Buford, a top guide on Calasawachahoochee Reservoir in Georgia and a widely traveled bass angler, has some advice on finding productive appliances. "Remember all those avocado–colored refrigerators and washers that people had in the sixties and seventies? Fish seem to like that color, kind of like my mother-in-law does. And so I scout neighborhoods near water, looking for older apartment complexes and housing developments where there's a lot of renovation work going on. Some of those avocado fridges or ovens or whatever always end up in the water, and a year later they're surrounded by fish."

Buford expresses considerable optimism for the future. In the 1990s, he notes, appliances with black enamel finishes achieved a degree of popularity. "Black's a perfect color for structure," he says, "and we should start to see some of those black ovens and refrigerators in the water over the next ten years. They'll be great places to find fish."

All the experts agree that an appliance without a door is more likely to hold fish than one with the door in place. The interior of a doorless washer or drier serves as an aquatic cave, a hiding place for bait or predators, whereas an intact appliance is little more than a big box lying on the bottom. "It really ticks me off when some yahoo dumps an oven or a washer with the door on it," Ben Kilgore says. "If that jerk had spent three minutes removing the hinge screws, he could have done something to improve the fishing. But I guess most people are just too lazy."

## HIDDEN RIGHT OUT IN THE OPEN

Every one of the guides with whom I fished made a similar comment: most fishermen simply fail to see the bounty all around them.

"Maybe it's just too obvious," says Gil Sanchez of real-world structure. "The average guy sees so many tires and appliances and car engines in the water that it just never occurs to him that these are great places to fish."

"I call it the 'back in the woods' mentality," Squint McGonigle explains. "A guy parks his car by the easiest public access to the water and figures that he's just got to go way back in the sticks to find some water that hasn't been fished to death. And so he ignores all the good structure right next to the road or under a bridge. What he doesn't realize is that everbody else is ignoring it, too, but the fish ain't. That guy doesn't know that he's got a gold mine within fifty feet of where he parks his car."

But now you know. Keep an eye peeled for Buick hoods, worn-out Goodyears, and stripped Chrysler V-8 blocks, and you can join a select group of anglers who understand the subtleties of modern fishing.

*Vermont, 2000*

## CHAPTER 12

# *Mackerel Jigs*

THE FISHING SLOWED DOWN CONSIDERABLY AFTER DICK BOATED HIS big striper. Up till then, we'd been enjoying pretty steady action with better-than-average schoolies, some of them within an inch or two of keeper size. It was pleasant, almost leisurely fly fishing, blind-casting big streamers from a comfortable boat on a flat-calm estuary. A bass would bust something on the surface every now and then, but we didn't see any of the concentrated topwater mayhem that induces fishermen to race from spot to spot chasing bait and game fish. The stripers were scattered and looking for food as the tide fell, so we took our time and made several long drifts through an area that Captain Greg knew would hold fish. I caught six or seven plump, hard-pulling schoolies, several on the better side of two feet, and Dick got at least that many.

Then a forty-three-inch bass ate Dick's fly, resented the trickery, and did its best to drag the seventeen-foot boat to the other side of the estuary. The fish peeled off a good eighty yards of backing, maybe more, before digging in for a stamina contest. It was an uncommonly determined fish, and it almost won. Dick was red in the face and pouring sweat by the time Captain Greg clamped the

Boga Grip on the striper's yap and hoisted it over the gunwale. The fly fell out the instant Dick touched it.

We took some pictures and had a beer to celebrate—ten o'clock really isn't too early when someone has caught a big fish—and then ran back to the head of the drift to have another go at the stripers. But we went biteless for the next half hour. Something had changed. The sun was higher, the tide was about done, and the fish had either split or gone off their feed.

The anglers, too, were about done, and maybe that's why the fish stopped cooperating. By ten-thirty, the temperature in the estuary must have been over ninety, and the dead-still air felt like a locker room without ventilation after an entire football team has showered. Although we hadn't been running around after busting fish, we'd been on the water since before sunrise, double-hauling long casts and fishing Captain Greg's huge, deer-hair-headed streamers with fast, jerky retrieves. Each us had thrown and stripped a couple miles of fly line. Dick's no youngster, and he looked pooped. I must have looked the same way—my increasingly sloppy casting was probably a clue—and when Greg suggested that we take a ride to see what we could find outside, beyond the jetty that guards the harbor, we didn't object. The good guides understand things besides finding fish.

I guess I'm just not a serious, high-performance fly fisherman, but one of the things I like best about saltwater angling is the chance to take a good boat ride. We stowed the rods, and Greg fired up the big Mercury. I felt cooler as soon as he had the boat up on plane. We skimmed across the flat estuary and over the little waves in the harbor, and then things got interesting as we ran past the jetty. I caught some spray in the face as the deep-V hull cut through the three-foot chop. Greg slowed down as we neared the big waves out at the mouth of the inlet, where the ocean fights with the estuary's flow. Anyone can run a boat fast, but it takes a good skipper to maneuver a small craft through seven- and eight-foot waves without shipping a drop of water or bouncing the passengers around. Greg handled the boat beautifully, alternately on and off the throttle as he negotiated the waves. And then we were outside.

The air was a good fifteen degrees cooler out on the deep water, with a light, steady breeze. We all perked up right away. Greg throttled back to trolling speed and switched on the depthfinder. I got up and stood next to him at the console to watch the numbers on the sonar unit change. The ocean rose and fell in long, smooth swells, rocking the boat just enough to make a landlubber like me bend his knees a little.

We chugged around for a while and even tried a few casts with outfits rigged with super-fast-sinking Teeny lines. Then Greg ran a little farther out, throttled back again, and began studying the depthfinder intently. It was a busy day off the coast of northern Massachusetts. Dozens of other fishing boats bobbed on the swells. Half a mile away, a party boat full of kids—a junior-high class trip, by the sounds of it—supplied a soundtrack.

We were in about ninety feet of water when Greg marked fish on the screen. A moment later, part of the depthfinder's screen went black as we began to pass over a dense school of something about thirty-five feet beneath the keel.

"Mackerel, probably," Greg said, tapping the screen. "Some big stuff, too, right on the bottom. Sharks, maybe, or cod. Who knows? Let's fish."

So we did, but thirty-five feet is a mite deep for fly fishing when there's a current running, even when you're casting a high-density line. But fly rods were all we had. We threw long casts with heavy flies and waited forever to let the lines sink before beginning a slow retrieve. Dick confirmed Greg's suspicions by catching a small mackerel after about ten minutes. I thought I felt a tug, but the slack in my line made it hard to tell. Another ten minutes passed without either of us getting a bite. Meanwhile, the sonar unit's screen remained black with fish that clearly had no inclination to come up even a few feet to eat our flies. I began to think about lunch.

"We should have brought a couple of conventional rods," Greg said.

As we continued heaving the fast-sinking lines as far as we could, hoping to gain an extra yard or two of depth on the retrieve, Greg rummaged around in the console, checking the contents of fly boxes. He found what he was looking for, pulled a small hook file out of the console, and spent a minute honing the hooks of a couple of shiny things. Then he looked up.

"Are you always 100 percent kosher?" he asked.

"Bubeleh," I said, "even if I weren't goyish, I'd eat a grilled cheese and bacon sandwich in a synagogue during a bris. Call me Mr. Practical. Watcha got?"

"Well, I got these little mackerel jigs," Greg said, showing me a couple of banana-shaped hunks of plated metal with hooks. "You can't cast them, of course, but they'll sure get down deep enough. I don't know how you feel about using hardware on a fly rod. Y'know, some guys . . ."

"I feel fine about it. I have neither pride nor shame. May I borrow one?" I was already clipping the fly from the leader as I spoke.

There's nothing like three-quarters of an ounce of metal for getting down in a hurry. I dropped the mackerel jig over the side. It went *bloop* and sank out of sight, pulling slack line through the guides.

"How deep?"

"Thirty-four feet," the captain said, studying the screen.

I fed out what I guessed was about thirty-five feet of specialized, expensive, high-performance fly line and began jigging with the $500 saltwater fly rod. Maybe ten seconds elapsed before the first mackerel ate the shiny jig, walloping the lure as I let it fall.

A mackerel, if I had to guess, consists of roughly 90 percent muscle and 10 percent panic. They are very fast fish. They have to be, because nearly everything in the ocean wants to eat them. Even a specimen less than a foot long, I learned, is loads of fun on a fly rod.

The mackerel zipped back and forth, changing directions wildly and putting a respectable bend in the rod tip as I stripped line. Mackerel don't know when to quit, either; this one kept swimming and thrashing after I lifted it from the water. Greg laughed as I tried to get a grip on the gyrating, slimy little fish. "Need the gaff?" he asked.

The mackerel went back into the sea, followed immediately by the jig. I wiped my slimy hands on my shirt as the lure sank, pumped the rod twice, and hooked another fish.

"You wanna try this special jigging rod?" I asked Dick as I played the second mackerel. "Seems to work real well." He indicated that he'd stick with a fly for the time being. He's a better, more serious fly fisher than I am, and I guess he has a reputation to uphold.

But there are benefits to having neither pride nor shame. In about three minutes, I caught another mackerel, then a foot-long pollock, then another mackerel, then a pollock. The pollock weren't as fast as the mackerel, but they pulled pretty well. I hadn't had this much simpleminded fun in a long time. By the time I released the seventh or eighth fish, my shirt must have smelled like a can of cheap cat food. Dick finally had enough of slinging around a 500-grain fly line and catching nothing—he had, after all, caught the day's best fish and had nothing to prove—and asked to try the jigging rod. I passed it back to him and rigged my 8-weight outfit with another of Greg's jigs.

For the next half hour we acted like a couple of half-bright kids who'd never seen fish, giggling and hollering as we pulled dozens of mackerel and pollock from the sea. A couple of the mackerel were just big and strong enough that I played them from the reel. The pollock made me wish I'd brought a cooler for the long ride home from Dick's place, because they're good to eat. We threw one mackerel in the boat's cooler for Dick's cat. Neither of us went more than a minute without a bite. We seemed to outfish the boats full of guys who knew what they were doing. We had the better guide.

Since we're pros with readers on at least four continents, we worked on improving the technique. A 9-foot, fast-action fly rod, we decided, makes a lousy jigging stick—too much give in the tip. We figured out that it was less tiring to tilt the rod downward and manipulate the lure by giving the line a fast, two-foot pull, and then letting it slide back out through the guides. The fish, we noted, nearly always took the jig as it dropped. Abrupt movements of the lure, we agreed, seemed more effective than a subtle action. Mackerel, we further agreed, are considerably slimier than pollock. More likely to bleed, too.

By the time we knocked off, my shirt and pants were stiff with fish slime and mackerel blood. My right index finger was rubbed raw from stripping line over it. My hands, I was sure, would attract cats for at least six months. And for once, I had caught enough fish. Sated and tired, grins creasing our sunburned mugs, we lolled in the boat as Greg steered us back to the inlet, through the big waves at the end of the jetty, and across the estuary baking under the noon sun. I nearly fell asleep in Greg's truck, like a little kid, on the ride back to Dick's house.

It was, to my way of thinking, a rare and perfect day. Challenges and technical fishing are all well and good in their place, and we'd had some while fly-casting to stripers in the estuary. One of us had caught a bragging-size fish, and that's always good. We had a fine boat ride and learned a few things from a skillful guide. But then we got really lucky and took advantage of a chance to act like ten-year-olds for an hour and come home reeking of good, clean, slimy fun.

I'll remember those mackerel and pollock, and jigging for them with a fancy fly rod and a hunk of shiny tin, for a long time. They reminded me of a couple of important fishing lessons. Always have a backup plan. And if you have a choice, pick a fly-fishing guide who keeps a few jigs in the console.

*South Carolina, 2002*

## CHAPTER 13

# *Breakfast Decisions*

"WOULD YOU EAT A TROUT," I ASKED MY SISTER ON FRIDAY NIGHT, "if I can get one worth cooking?" She and my brother-in-law had come up from New Jersey for a weekend visit.

*"Yes,"* she said, and smacked her lips. "Yum. I haven't had a *real* trout in so long."

A real trout is one caught by our dad or me. Later, we figured that Karen hadn't eaten one in more than twenty-five years.

When she was little, though, my sister ate a lot of trout. From April through June, Dad and I fished the local brooks at least two mornings or evenings a week, and we also made a few trips to bigger water an hour away. We fished sometimes with flies, more often with little worms that we roll-cast with soft fiberglass fly rods. The limit was six trout apiece, and on many mornings we killed a dozen between us.

Weekend mornings when we fished locally were best. We'd get home by nine or nine-thirty, dirty and stinky and toting a creel full of trout. Mom would flee her kitchen, asking us *please* not to make the mess she knew we'd make anyway, and Dad would make breakfast. Dad's skills as a chef are meager—his specialty when Karen and I were kids was leftover spaghetti warmed up in a big frying pan—but cooking the kill is man's work. He'd fry bacon in one pan, canned potatoes in another, and trout in a third, while Karen or I buttered the slices as they popped up from the toaster. Within twenty minutes, the kitchen was awash in spilled and splattered grease; within thirty, we'd consumed enough cholesterol to make a cardiologist weep. But no king ever ate better.

By the time she was seven years old, Karen was adept at picking apart a trout, using two tiny fondue forks to lift the meat from the whiskery bones. She'd eat an entire fish, sometimes part of a second. When Dad pointed out that the best part is the chunk of muscle in the cheek (and it is), Karen would make a face and say, "But it's next to the *eye*," and Dad would laugh. As we finished eating, Mom would look aghast at the wreckage and wonder aloud if burning the place down and starting over might make more sense than trying to clean up. But we'd put things to rights eventually, after which Dad and I would retire to the living room for a snooze.

Then I got older and things changed. I didn't fish much during college, preferring to devote evenings to loud music and girls, and mornings to hangovers. Within a few years, Dad stopped fishing for trout. He'd become passionate about skeet shooting, and later, he bought the first of a series of motorboats. After the age of eleven or twelve, Karen had no more trout for breakfast.

Now, more than a quarter of a century later, I wanted very much to catch a trout for my little sister. I think we needed to reach back and grab something from childhood. Our mother's illness had finally forced her into an assisted-living facility from which we knew she would not come home. Dad had taken care of her as long as he could, and now, shattered and exhausted, he had to let his wife, high-school sweetheart, and childhood playmate slip away, and there was little anyone could do to help either of them. Only weeks after Mom had left her home, Mary Jo and I had deposited our younger daughter at a college far away, and our home's sudden silence overwhelmed us.

The years seemed very heavy that summer, and they seemed to be going by much too goddamn fast. Maybe it wasn't fair to ask some poor little brook trout to shoulder the weight or put the brakes on time, but I nominated one for the job anyway.

"Okay," I said, "I'll try to catch a trout or two tomorrow or Sunday morning."

These days, of course, killing a trout is a serious matter, at least in fly-fishing circles. Dad and I used to slaughter scores of them every spring, but that was a different time, and the fish came from a hatchery. I proposed to go to the little stream behind our condo and wantonly kill wild brookies. Many of the people who read the stuff I edit and write would rather see me piss on the pope or lob a pipe bomb at the Dalai Lama. Politically correct fly-fishing magazines no longer run pictures of dead trout. Print a photo of a guy with his fingers in a trout's gills, and you get hate mail from readers.

I hadn't kept a trout in at least five years, partly because putting them back had long ago become a habit, and partly because catch-and-release angling is just plain easier. I've given up making the life-or-death decision every time I go fishing. All my hooks are barbless, and I no longer carry a net or creel. If I land a fish, fine; if it comes unstuck first, that's just as good.

But releasing a fish is, for me, a conservation decision, not an act of piety—an ethical matter, perhaps, but not a moral choice in regard to that one fish. If I want to kill a trout and eat it, that's just too bad for that fish. For the moment, my intelligence and ability to use tools have put me on a higher link of the food chain. If I release the fish, I do it so that you or I might catch it again, so that it can breed more fish for me and you to catch, because I know that we anglers can collectively kill fish more quickly than they can reproduce, or because I simply don't want to go to the trouble of cleaning and cooking it. Turning a fish loose is a resource-management decision, and nothing more. I'm not that hungry for fish anyway.

Not everyone sees it that way, of course. Years ago, at a conservation-group meeting, an acquaintance told me, with a straight face, that keeping a trout is the moral equivalent of killing a person. For this bloke, a devout fly fisher, trout are sacred animals—totems, in effect—and consigning one to the frying pan is morally wrong, a *sin* just like murder or adultery. He hopes someday to see laws prohibiting any sort of fishing but the kind he does.

The foolishness of such thinking hardly merits comment. The disciples of catch-and-release fanaticism overlook its dangers. Once we make killing an individual trout a moral issue, a sin, we might eventually conclude that sticking a metal hook in its yap so that we can watch the fish jump is wrong. And then where would we be? Besides, if my acquaintance were small enough, a trout would eat *him* in a heartbeat and not worry about the morality of it.

Sporting ethics is a strange and selectively logical branch of philosophy. I once got into a discussion of the subject with a fishing writer, and he pulled me up short with a simple question: "What, exactly, are the ethics of inflicting pain, terror, and death for one's own amusement?" You have to dance around that one, because it's a tough question to tackle head-on.

And dance around it we do. Our treatment of animals is hardly ever rational. To shoot a woodcock is okay; to kill a mockingbird is not. Some folks make pets of bunnies; others blast them with shotguns. Get caught catching a deer in a big leg-hold trap and you'll go to jail—but you're allowed to shoot a razorhead arrow between the animal's ribs so that it drowns in its own blood. We in the West are revolted by the idea of eating dogs, but other cultures don't hesitate to put old Duke on a spit. Divine law forbids pork to Jews and Moslems, yet God-fearing Baptists stuff themselves with swine at the Sunday barbecue. The Hindu shudders at our love of cheeseburgers but wouldn't mind trying our fried chicken. Only the Buddhist who forswears all killing seems consistent. But he never gets to go fishing or hunting, so he's clearly crazy.

I'm as nonrational as the next guy. I can kill a trout or catfish without a qualm, but I will not keep a bass. Worms and minnows are bait, and I impale them on hooks without a second thought. But I still feel bad about the one frog that I used as bait many years ago. There's no explanation; it's just how I'm built.

The animal-rights crazies (and the most extreme catch-and-release zealots) are all wet when they suggest that a trout occupies the same moral or metaphysical plane that I do. Whether God gave me dominion over the beasts or evolution put me on a higher link of the food chain, my killing and eating are part of the natural order of things. The trout eats the mayflies, I eat the trout, and if I drop dead on the riverbank, the bugs, worms, microbes, birds, and animals will eat me. That's how it works. Nature is supremely indifferent. You're a predator until you can't cut the mustard anymore, and then you're lunch.

There's no getting away from the bloody part of blood sport, even in catch-and-release fly fishing. That a fish feels anything like our sensation of pain, as the animal-rights loonies believe, seems ludicrous to me. Look at the things fish eat. A smallmouth bass or a trout will suck in a live crayfish that has a hard shell and powerful claws. Since the crawdad resents becoming food, it fights back. The fish crushes the hapless crustacean to a pulp in its throat, and then swallows it. A bonefish will do the same thing with a mantis shrimp, a critter equipped with forelimbs so strong that it earned the nickname "thumb buster." I would pay money to watch an animal-rights extremist put a live crayfish or mantis shrimp—or a hellgrammite or bumblebee—into his mouth, hold it for a few seconds, swallow it, and then, assuming he can still speak, tell me that a fish's yap has the same sensations as mine. Eating cannot be painful; survival forbids it.

Clearly, though, a bass or trout is not delighted when I set the hook. It pulls one way while I pull the other. It swims and jumps and thrashes while I whoop and holler. Sometimes a fish dies because I have hooked it deep in the throat or in the gills. Does my pleasure, this bone-deep and almost spiritual happiness that comes from fishing, rest on some creature's suffering or death?

Maybe it does, sometimes. I have to just accept that. Try as I might, I cannot rationalize my need to fish, cannot justify the things I do with hooks. In the end, there's no explaining blood sport. Some of us have to fish or hunt. Just plain have to.

Maybe the healthiest and most honest attitude is one expressed by a conservation writer with whom I had a long chat some years ago. "Once a year," he told me, "I have to go kill an elk with a bow and arrow. Tough shit." And then he gets on with life.

That works. Unless, of course, you're the elk. Or, in the case of my decision, a trout.

But I'm not the trout, and so I had little trouble deciding to catch breakfast for my sister.

It was rainy and windy Saturday morning, and I put off the trout hunt. Sunday morning was clear and calm. I got up a little after dawn and crept out the back door while everyone else was still asleep.

The little brook is one of the headwaters of an undeservedly famous trout stream. Farther down, just above where it joins another branch, it probably holds a few browns. Behind the condo we rented, it's strictly brook-trout water, and not very fertile brook-trout water. If you fish it hard and well, you might pound up half a dozen fish in a morning. An eight-incher is a trophy. It doesn't contain a whole lot of food, it floods violently and freezes deep, and it doesn't afford its trout much of a living. It's pretty, but harsh and treacherous, like the country through which it flows.

Our deck overlooked the best pool, a surprisingly deep hole that you need chest waders to cross. For the sake of the view, the condo management had cleared a hundred-foot patch of marshy ground along the bank, creating a gap in the thick brush and making a nice spot for casting into the deep pool. Except for that one brush-hogged clearing directly behind our unit, the brook is little more than a watery tunnel through a jungle, and very tough to fish.

I moseyed down the right side of the clearing, toting a light, 8-foot rod and keeping close to the brush. There was no point in thinking about hatches this late in the year, so I'd tied one of my magic rubber ants to the 5X tippet. It was a chilly morning, one of those that says that the brief New England summer has about run its course, the kind that makes you start looking for some color in the trees.

Ten feet from the water, I stopped and studied the pool for a while. Habit. Nothing rose, because nothing had a reason to. Maybe a nymph would make more sense, I thought. But the ant always worked. I could switch to a nymph after a couple dozen casts. As softly as I could, I walked down to the bank.

The bottom comes up quickly at the foot of the pool, forming an abrupt, fast tailout that never holds a fish. The deep water a few yards above the tailout looks promising, but it almost always disappoints. Wild brook trout go through life with a bad case of nerves, and maybe they feel too exposed in the calm water in the middle of the pool.

I made a few short casts to the deepest water and raised one tiddler, a four-inch runt that came unstuck a heartbeat after taking the ant. Then I lengthened my casts and made a dozen drifts where the choppy water of the chute begins to smooth out. Usually, this spot holds at least one fish. Not today.

Fishing for meat changes the game, of course, and suddenly I wanted very much, almost desperately, to return to the condo with at least one hunk of flesh on a stick. Catching always beats not catching, but today it *mattered* whether I caught a trout. Even as I took a few steps upstream so that I could begin to work the chute, it occurred to me how happy I am not to fish in bass tournaments, where every fish, every day, matters.

The chute is on the left side of the pool as you face upstream. It's the outside of a thirty-foot-long curve the brook makes as the water tumbles downhill through a short, violent riffle and into the hole where it becomes a pool. In spots, the chute probably comes up to my thighs. I'm not sure of the depth because I've never waded the chute's full length; the current is too powerful and the bottom too uneven.

You wouldn't think that fish could hold in that strong flow, or, even if they could, that they'd want to. But the big rocks on the ankle-twisting bottom create pockets of slack water a yard below the surface, and the brook trout lie in the pockets. They have to swim hard to come out of their holes, grab a bug, and get back to safety before the current sweeps them down into the pool. But they do it. They have spirit, these trout.

A dead tree lies in the shallow water on the right side of the brook, a few of its branches hanging within a foot of the chute. Another tree hangs over the middle of the pool, the tips of its limbs behind you as you fish the chute. And so you have to watch both ends of the cast, letting neither the backcast nor the delivery stray too far to your right. I've left a few flies in the tree over the pool, and probably a dozen in the dead tree that guards the chute.

It's easiest to cast if you kneel on the bank, and that's what I did, with the rod angled so that the line passed over my head. You don't get much of a drift in the chute—two feet, maybe three before the fly starts to drag and you have to strip hard and throw a quick roll cast to get the line back in the air for the next presentation. It's some of the most tiring fishing I've ever done with only fifteen feet of line out of the rod. Somehow, though, the brookies see a little black ant racing by on the rough water and come up to get it before it vanishes.

One came up on my second cast into the chute. It made a little boil on the choppy surface and sent a spurt of water into the air. I flicked the rod up and the fish swam upstream, boring into the current with enough oomph to bend the tip section. Then it angled toward the shallow water and turned sideways, letting the current carry it downstream into the pool, where it dug in and added the current's strength to its own. But even with the stream's help, of course, it wasn't strong enough.

It was a good fish by the standards of the brook, maybe eight inches long and more plump than most. I held it for a moment, admiring its colors and all the little teeth in its oversize mouth. A first-rate predator, the brook trout. Then I killed it and laid it on the grass.

I fished the rest of the chute and raised another fish, but missed it when I struck. I looked up toward the condo and saw my wife on the deck in her bathrobe, watching me. We waved to each other. It was almost breakfast time.

I'd brought a little folding knife, a frighteningly sharp thing I'd bought years before and hadn't used more than half a dozen times. But my hands hadn't forgotten how to clean a trout, and I slit the brookie's belly from vent to gills, hooked an index finger through the gills, and pulled out gills and guts in one messy, bloody piece. I threw the innards into the brook. Something would eat them. Then I scraped out the fish's kidney, rinsed the trout, my hands, and the knife in the brook, and walked up the hill to our back door.

Karen and Rich were at the table working on the day's first cup of coffee.

"Want a trout?" I asked.

"You got one?" Her eyes lit up.

"Of *course* I got one," I said, playing Big Brother the Mighty Slayer of Beasts. "Fish are powerless to resist my magic flies."

I cooked the trout the old way, the way Dad taught me, and the only way I've ever cooked one. Sprinkle the inside of the body with a little coarse-ground black pepper and a pinch of paprika, then pan-fry the fish in sweet butter. Give it a couple of minutes on the first side, even less time on the second side. When the skin peels off easily, the fish is done.

While the trout sizzled, I warmed up a plate on top of the toaster oven and found a couple of little fondue forks in the miscellaneous-utensils drawer.

"It smells like when we were little," Karen said.

She ate the fish just as she had eaten others thirty years before, peeling back the skin and using the little forks to slide the meat off the bones. Rich tried a piece, and Karen gave a tiny chunk to Ringo the cat. We laughed about the only cat in town that had fresh brook trout for breakfast.

Then we talked about the time Dad shot several pheasants when we were kids. Mom cooked them, and we had a pheasant dinner punctuated by the occasional crunch of a No. 6 shot between someone's molars. Thrifty housewife that she was, our mother saved the leftovers. The next day she made sandwiches, one of which Karen took to school.

At noon, when her classmates began the daily ritual of comparing lunch-bag contents, Karen sat silent. One girl noted that she had peanut butter and jelly. Another had bologna, again. A third had liverwurst.

"*I* have pheasant," Karen said when the other girls had finished talking. It was the only time either of us ever humbled an entire lunch table.

I sat and drank a cup of coffee while my sister ate her trout and made *yum* sounds, the kitchen smelling of burned butter and my hands smelling faintly of trout slime. Once upon a time, before we knew confusion and grief, when our parents were young, the world had in its best moments smelled and tasted like this. The brook behind our condo, like all brooks, like all water, had for a few minutes focused my life into perfect clarity, and a trout sizzling in a frying pan had let my sister and me almost forget that thirty years had gone by.

It seemed, and still seems, a righteous killing and a worthy end for a brook trout.

*Vermont, 2001*

## CHAPTER 14

# *A Box of Hope*

IT'S FUNNY WHEN AN EDITOR WHO HAS LITTLE INTEREST AND LESS faith in stories about new flies and lures nonetheless spends a lot of time and more than a little money making new flies and lures. After editing, writing, or reading hundreds of articles and dozens of books about flies, I've come to regard the lot as twaddle. At least half are merely grist for the mill: magazines need cover lines and tackle companies need ads that say, "Hot New Flies!" Of the remainder, some are perpetrated by guys looking to build a reputation, and others are the work of well-meaning chaps who don't know that their amazing new creations were sold, under different names, fifty years ago. Very, very few of the breakthrough-in-fly-design articles describe anything within shouting distance of newness, and even they are largely irrelevant—solutions in search of problems, as a friend puts it.

Sure, most of this year's crop of new lures and flies might actually catch a fish. So will last year's stuff, and the junk Grandpa fished with back when Coolidge occupied the White House. By and large, innovations in angling exist so that someone can sell something. Companies sell new products to fishermen; magazines sell advertising space to companies and stories to readers. Famous fishermen stay famous, manufacturers stay busy, editors fill issues, anglers have new toys. It's a beautiful system. Of course, when you've been inside the system for a while, or if you're a perceptive observer, you might come to regard the latest, hottest, most energetically hyped flies and lures with less than childlike faith.

Don't misunderstand. I would not imply that fishing writers ever indulge in fiction or that editors can reach such depths of cynicism as not to care whether the work they print is every bit as literally true as, say, the Old Testament.

But think about this for minute. If magazine stories about flies and lures serve tawdry commercial purposes, they are worthless nonsense. If every one of them is true, then the sheer annual volume and collective contradictions of such articles suggest that damn near anything will catch a fish at one time or another, and the stories are again nonsense. And if some articles are true and some are claptrap, we're left with the challenge of figuring out which is which. Better to stick with a Muddler Minnow, Royal Coachman, purple plastic worm, diving plug, or a fat shiner impaled on a hook, and let the subscriptions lapse.

I know these things. And yet, I toil mightily at the workbench, crafting new lures and flies. My output over the past decade would have stocked a small tackle store, and still I keep making things with hooks in them. I enjoy buying the parts and materials that will become flies and lures in my hands, and I await the arrival of an order like a kid waiting for Christmas morning.

As I write this, a baker's dozen of new, utterly unnecessary flies lies on the table next to me, waiting for the next smallmouth-bass expedition. On a stool beneath the table sits a six-inch-thick stack of catalogs offering rod blanks and rod-building components I cannot in good conscience buy until I sell a few more of the rods already gathering dust on the other side of the room. On a bead-chain rack behind me hang several recently finished spinnerbaits and a buzzbait, soon to join four dozen of their brethren in the trunk of my car. Metal shelves, big plastic bins, and three office cabinets contain God knows how many dollars' worth of fly-tying materials, hooks, lure parts, and special tools. And that's just in this room. The bedroom closet holds more rods and reels, equally large plastic tubs full of fly boxes and lures, and a specialized tool kit for reel maintenance.

With only a little sophistry, I can justify some of my junk. The tools and fly-tying materials were amortized long ago, and at this point I probably do save money by tying flies. Indeed, if I didn't build rods and tie flies and make lures, I couldn't afford to fish. Not well, anyway.

But the real reasons I maintain stocks of mottled brown hen feathers and aluminum buzzbait blades, the true justifications for my boxes of fly-tying thread and spinnerbait skirts, have nothing to do with finances and, sometimes, little to do with catching fish that I intend to throw back anyway. I *like* all this stuff and the things I make with it; knowing how to make lures and flies and rods gives me a deep, abiding satisfaction.

Tackle tinkerers search for lofty, intellectual justifications for their hobby, but I think we can start with the simple pleasures of making. What you make doesn't matter; the point is merely to make something. Once upon a time, that might not have been as true. Nowadays, though, our homes are filled with appliances and electronic gadgets bearing labels that say, "No user-serviceable parts inside." Those stickers might as well go on the hoods of cars, too. Perhaps radios with tubes and ignition systems with breaker points were, objectively, inferior to their contemporary counterparts, but you could fix them when they went wrong and take satisfaction in the job. That's all gone now.

With computers, most of us have regressed to an age of magic. If we perform certain rituals, desired results occur. How and why they occur are unknown and, practically speaking, unknowable. Taking the thing apart affords no clues to a mind such as mine; my computer contains no cams and pushrods, no chains and sprockets. I double-click on an icon (note the word) labeled "Browse the Internet," and moments later I'm looking at a fishing catalog on a website in England. The website isn't tangible, and neither is the Internet, and I don't have the faintest idea what really *happens* when I double-click a picture of an arrow on another picture that exists only as some excited atoms inside a cathode-ray tube. If that's not magic, I don't know what is. We might as well rattle bones and poke around in chicken entrails.

The world becomes steadily less tangible and user-serviceable. We make, repair, or even understand fewer of the things we use. Small wonder, then, that handicrafts—woodworking, pottery, model-airplane building, fancy cookery—grow in popularity. Building a bookcase or a radio-controlled toy plane serves a need left unfulfilled by computers and CD players and automobiles that only specialists dare take apart.

Humans make things or go crazy. Humans who fish make flies, lures, rods, nets, and even the tools and gadgets that make the making possible. When I put the guides on a fly rod, I use wrapping stands and a thread-tension device that I built, and I revel in the double craftsmanship.

To pick just the right feather from a brown hen cape is to exercise judgment acquired through experience, and to turn the hackle into the elegant, swept-back collar of a wet fly is to employ skills and dexterity that 99 percent of the populace will never have. There's satisfaction in knowing that a spinnerbait made with one big Colorado blade will swim higher in the water than another built with a pair of willowleaf blades. It feels good to fold the wet-fly hackle as you wrap it, to bend the wire of the spinnerbait's arm to make a neat loop for the swivel.

There's satisfaction, too, in knowing that your handiwork is unique. Fly tiers love the word *pattern,* but each of us leaves his stamp on every fly he ties, even the old standards.

When I worked in the jewelry trade, my employers and I some-times forgot which of us had made a particular piece. The boss, Bia-gio, would remove a ring from the display case and ask me, "Did you make this, or did my brother Michael?"

"I think you made it, didn't you? With one of those sapphires you got from that Arab guy last winter?"

"Nope, it's not mine," Biagio would say, studying the prongs through his loupe. "I remember getting those stones, but this isn't my work. I think it's yours. Here, look." And he'd hand me the ring so I could study it.

"Michael did this," I'd say after examining the piece. "He doesn't cut the prongs as deep as I do, and he leaves less gold on top of the stone. He did a really nice job with this one. Look at the tops of the prongs and you'll see what I mean." And back the ring would go to Biagio.

"Yeah, you're right. You and Michael do some stuff a lot alike. But this is his. Your prongs are more heavy-duty."

We were looking at things invisible to the naked eye, details of metal work and tiny tool marks we could see through a 10X jeweler's loupe, and which a layman wouldn't spot with twice as much magni-fication. All three of us set stones well, mounting them so that the setting would withstand considerable abuse, yet each of us had a style, a signature left in the little fingers of gold that held a sapphire or ruby or diamond. We took pride in it, and in being able to tell our styles apart.

It's the same with tying flies and making lures. I learned to rec-ognize the styles of my contributors from the flies they sent with articles. One guy made the body of a Light Cahill a fraction of a mil-limeter fatter; another tied the pattern with slightly fuller wings; a third habitually used a few more fibers in the tail; another left a whisker's breadth of bare shank behind the hook eye. Fish don't care about such things, but fly tiers do.

My spinnerbaits and trout flies and homemade rods don't look exactly like those you can buy in stores. Maybe mine are better, maybe they're not. They're *mine,* and that's the point of making them.

I tie flies and make lures year-round, but the pace and purpose of my work change with the seasons. From early spring until early fall, I tie flies to replace those broken off in trees or wrecked by fish, or because I have an idea I want to try tomorrow. I paint and assemble lures to fill holes in the assortment—maybe I'm getting low on black and purple spinnerbaits, or I wonder if the bass would like a yellow and green, quarter-ounce buzzbait with a shorter, sparser skirt. During the fishing season, I work in a hurry, knocking out two or three flies or a single lure to get me through the next day or week. There's fishing to be done, and there isn't time for mass production or my best craftsmanship.

During the cold months, when the ponds are frozen and the streams two-thirds covered by ice, I might tell myself that I'm restocking the boxes or preparing a new, bigger, better arsenal for next season. Maybe I tie a dozen dry flies exactly like one another, or give ten spinnerbait heads an extra two coats of clear gloss finish. Although 80 percent of last year's spinnerbait-caught bass fell to the single, size 4 Colorado blade, I make a few new lures with different arrangements; one gets a tandem-blade rig, sizes 2 and 3 (it should run just a little deeper than the solo size 4 blade), and another, on a whim, gets a size 3 blade in front of a size 4 (that'll make ferocious vibrations, I tell myself). I fill a few fly-box compartments with variations of last year's killers, and then another few with variations of the variations. When I build rods, I do it during the winter and take twice as long on each one as I have to.

Sure, I'll use the stuff—some of it, anyway—but what I'm really doing is getting as close to going fishing as I can. As I bend the spinnerbait wires or tie the silicone-rubber skirts, divide the wings on a dry fly or dub a thorax on a nymph, fit a cork handle to a rod blank or dress the feet of the snake guides, my eyes see a trout jump, my ears hear clear water tumbling over stones, my nose smells bedding bluegills on a warm spring evening, my right hand feels a fly rod's thumping grip, my left hand strains against the handle of a plug rod with a fat old she-bass at the end of the line.

Snowplows and shovels and ice scrapers are not really the tools that beat back the winter. That job belongs to the fly-tying vise, wire-bending pliers, and rod-wrapping stands. Where they are, spring is, too.

Summer or winter, I fill plastic boxes with hope and wrap anticipation around rod blanks. I know it's all silly. Only an even bigger fool than I would bet a nickel that the new rod will make me cast farther or more accurately. Fifty spinnerbaits are plenty, even if some are kind of beat up; I do not need another two dozen, and I shall not catch one additional bass for having them. The trout ate foam-rubber ants last summer, and they'll eat them again next year, and yet I tie not only four times as many ants as I'll need, but all sorts of other flies, too. Half of the new, lovingly hackled drys will never get wet; the hooks of two-thirds of the experimental wet flies will rust from humidity before they ever swim in a stream. I probably will *not* find occasion to use 4-inch-long Deceivers that look (to me, anyway) like trout-stream minnows, and I must have been half crocked when I tied those eight ludicrously complex crayfish flies. And, God help me, I even devoted most of a weekend to carving and painting three wooden bass plugs that probably won't have any action.

If I had to justify all this stuff, all this work, and all this money to a judge with life-and-death powers, I'd end up with a noose around my neck. *Nolo contendere,* Your Honor; fetch the hangman and I'll give him a few tips on knots.

I know it's all crazy—but only in the rational, workaday part of my noggin. The fishing part of me says that I must do these things because maybe I'll find some combination of nickel-plated blades and rubber skirt that will catch the seven-pound bass my gut tells me lives in the pond, or perhaps (you never know) the new 8-weight stick will help me push a striper fly six feet farther into the wind, or it could be that the subtle improvements in this year's nymphs will dupe trout that spurned last year's models.

Yes, this one—this rod, this buzzbait, this deer-hair bug, this dry fly with tails forked just so—will get 'em. In the months and weeks and days before I use it, I know, with religious certainty, that the new and as-yet-untried plug rod, spinnerbait, or streamer fly will have powerful magic, wonderful powers that I gave it. Next year will be better.

Every now and then, events partly justify my faith. The black spinnerbaits raised hell for one season, and the little 5-weight built with a cheap, private-label blank turned out to be a very fine trout rod. Mostly, though, all the hours and dollars buy hope, not results; the stuff I make catches no end of fish in my head, but puts far fewer in my hand.

But I can fill out another mail-order form, put another hook in the vise, open another bottle of vinyl jig paint, attach new spinnerbait blades to new swivels, make reel-seat bushings on a new rod blank. With a few feathers or some new stripping guides or forty strands of silicone rubber, I can make spring come whenever I want.

Hope does indeed spring eternal, if you know how to work with the parts.

*Vermont, 2001*

## CHAPTER 15

# Sketches
# of Noteworthy Anglers

I HADN'T HEARD THE KID APPROACHING, PROBABLY BECAUSE HE stepped out of a Norman Rockwell painting and simply materialized on the bank of the stream. Mark Twain might have had such a kid in mind when he wrote *Tom Sawyer*. You don't see many such essentially boyish boys these days. The world gets ahold of kids too early, turning them into cynics or thugs or larval yuppies, teaching them avarice or anger or sadness much too early. Or maybe, fifteen years later, I'm just closer to curmudgeonhood than I suspect.

He was wearing rolled-up dungarees and high-top canvas sneakers and carrying an ultralight spinning rod and a small plastic tackle box. He stood watching me cast in the Mayor's Pool for a while, and I let him. I turned and said hello, and he said hello back. I went back to casting. Another minute passed.

"Hey mister," he said. "Do you know where the fish are?"

Ah, the eternal question. He got right to the point, this kid. But I wasn't sure I liked the sound of "mister." At thirty, it was the first time I'd heard the word applied to me.

"Well, do you mean generally or specifically?" I asked. "What I mean is, are you asking where fish are in general, or where they are in this particular river?"

"Yeah, that's it. Do you know where the fish are *here?*"

I noted that I generally managed to find a couple, but admitted that I hardly ever knew where all the fish were.

"Well, I'll tell you," the kid said. And he did. For ten minutes he jabbered at me, pointing upstream and down, describing places and features, naming fish and the things they'd bite. You'd have thought he was an outdoor writer but for his patent sincerity. I stood there agog, my fly line trailing in the current.

It was all nonsense, of course, compounded equally of fantasy, misinformation, and whatever gibberish the kid had picked up from fishing magazines. He attributed great depth to places I knew were shin deep, put prodigious fish in spots where I'd never seen so much as a chub, assigned fish that didn't even live in the stream to places where the species wouldn't be found in any case, and stocked barren stretches of the crummy little river with both trophy largemouth bass and jumbo rainbow trout.

But you couldn't fault his enthusiasm and generosity. He told me where to catch the six-pound bass (in a stream where a twelve-inch smallmouth was a once-a-decade fish), where to find the biggest "native" trout (in a stream that got warm enough in the summer to kill most of the stockers), and where to look for the giant pike that ate baby ducks and muskrats (in water that had never even held a good pickerel).

He finally stopped, grinning, clearly proud to have shared his secrets. I asked him to repeat one or two points, and he did, with zest and clarity. I thanked him and stripped in my line to check my fly.

The kid waited a minute while I replaced my nymph with another.

"Are you gonna stay here?" he asked. Maybe he was surprised, or disappointed, that I wasn't rushing off to try the much better water he'd described.

"Well, yeah, for a while," I said. "I usually catch something in the head of this pool, up in the fast water."

"Oh. Okay. Well, I'm gonna go upstream. Good luck. Don't forget about those places I told you about."

I assured him I wouldn't. And off he went, oozing confidence, knowing just where to find the fierce pike, the big brookies, the meanest bass, the fastest rainbows, the largest perch, the fattest browns, the giant bluegills. He strode away in his high-tops, a boy with a mission, a guy walking through a whole world of happy illusions.

Good for you, I thought. Don't let the world get ahold of you too soon.

We'd had a soggy spring, and the river was running a bit high for comfortable fly fishing. But I had a free morning, and so I fished, leaning into the current to keep my footing in the fast stretches, inching my way out from the flooded bank until I had room for a backcast, struggling and generally failing to get a good drift with a nymph, shipping water over the tops of my hip boots several times. It was a bright, clear day full of the promise of summer, and I didn't mind getting wet and not catching fish.

I eyeballed the narrow stretch of pocket water that was usually good for a few smallmouths in July, but decided to pass it up as too fast and rough. Above the pocket water, the river curved through a long stretch of rapids, and above the rapids was a deep, fast run under an old railroad bridge. The run was impossible to fish with a fly rod except when the water was very low. But the path widened into a level clearing under one side of the trestle, and that spot usually held something amusing. It was a gathering place and trysting spot for local teenagers, and on any summer morning you could usually find an astonishing number of empty beer bottles strewn around the remains of a campfire. As often as not, you could spot a pair of panties and sometimes a bra hanging from a nail on the underside of the wooden bridge. Once I found three pairs of knickers adorning the underpinnings. It was good to know that the youngsters were having fun.

On this morning, though, my attention was snagged by a guy sitting on the middle of the railroad bridge, right above the center of the run. He was a young, skinny Hispanic chap, and he was fishing. Actually, he was sitting, with a huge surf rod lying next to him on one side and a small cooler occupying the spot on his other side. He had a bottle of beer in one hand and a smile of utter contentment on his face.

He waved and called hello. I said hello back.

"You fishin' too, huh? You get anything?" he asked.

I admitted the futility of my efforts.

"I got one so far," he said, and held up a trout on a stringer.

I congratulated him.

"You want a beer, man?" he asked, gesturing toward the little cooler.

"No, thanks. Kind of early for me." It was about nine o'clock.

"Nah, man, it's not too early. The birds are singing and the bees are buzzing and, like, all that nature shit, man." He was starting to sound like a cut from an old Cheech and Chong album. "It's a beautiful day. I come out here with my fishin' pole and a six-pack of Bud and maybe I get some fish and maybe I don't, but it doesn't matter. It's just beautiful to be out here, man. It's never too early for a beer on a beautiful day when you're fishin'."

He was sitting in creosote on a rickety railroad bridge that crossed a shabby little river, eight feet above a pile of broken beer bottles and used condoms and other refuse of the active teenage lifestyle, five minutes in one direction from a moribund industrial

burg full of tenements and abandoned stores, ten minutes in another
direction from one of the nation's most hellish suburban highways,
fishing for stocked trout with a surf rod, knocking back the first
brewski of the day at nine in the morning. And he was, by all
appearances, the happiest man in Christendom.

The tip of his surf rod twitched. He put down his beer, carefully,
and winched up another trout, which joined its brother on the
stringer. His terminal tackle consisted of a fluke rig with a small
pyramid sinker and what looked like about a size 6 bait hook. He
impaled a fresh night crawler on the hook—he kept the bait in the
cooler with his beer—and dropped the rig back into the run. Then
he set the rod down by his side, finished his beer, and opened
another.

"What are you fishin' with, man?"

"Flies," I said.

"You mean, like, bugs and shit? What do you do, catch them and
then stick them on a hook or something?"

"Well, no. They're fake bugs."

"Fake bugs? Far out. Do they, like, sell them in bait stores or
something?"

"Sometimes. I make my own."

"Wow. You *make* fake bugs? That's intense, man. And fish eat
them? That's pretty cool. *Fake* bugs. But you ain't caught nothin' yet
today. Better get busy, man, before I catch them all." He laughed.
"You sure you don't want a beer? I got four more, man. No problem."

"Maybe later," I said, and we parted.

I worked my way upstream for an hour or so, looking for spots
where I could wade and water slow enough that I could manage a
drift. I caught a chub in a stretch where the river became wide, slow,
and shallow, and then started back downstream.

My friend was still sitting on the bridge. But now he was
singing. The six-pack, I was willing to bet, was pretty much gone. I

wondered if he got up and walked to the edge of the bridge when he had to take a leak, picking his tipsy way from one rotten tie to the next, or if he simply peed in the river. I passed under the bridge and came into his field of view.

"Too late, man," he sang out, and laughed. 'This is my last beer. You took too long. But I got six trout." He held the stringer aloft. "Six beers, six trout. The limit's the same as a six-pack. You think they did that deliberately? I mean, if the limit was, like, twelve fish, and you drank two six-packs, you'd be too fucked up to get home and eat your fish, you know?" He laughed again. Then he asked if I got anything.

One chub, I admitted.

"That sucks, man. You still using those fake bugs? You should try worms, man. And a big sinker. But it's still a beautiful day. Well, I gotta go home. My mom and dad will be glad to see these fish."

As he walked away along the old railroad tracks, weaving a little, surf rod and stringer of trout in one hand and a cooler full of empty bottles in the other, I had no doubt whose side God was on that beautiful day.

Fifty-plus years' worth of unfiltered Chesterfields had given the old guy a voice as raspy as the clicker of cheap fly reel that hadn't been greased in a decade. I used to run into him at least a couple times a month on the little river we shared with too many other folks, and though we always exchanged greetings and had half a dozen conversations over the course of two trout seasons, I never learned his name. I've always figured it was Humphrey, but that his friends called him Red.

He had an old, yellow fiberglass rod, a Wright & McGill Sweetheart, the handle black with use and the wraps three different colors because he'd replaced the guides one at a time as they wore or got damaged over the years, using whatever ancient spool of rod-winding thread he found first. I used to imagine him going into the huge sporting-goods store in the next town every spring and buying one snake guide. A small, battered Medalist, its black finish mostly gone, occupied the Sweetheart's reel seat. I know that Red fished a double-taper line because he told me during one of our chats. Weight-for-ward lines, he explained, were just another ripoff designed to appeal to overinflated egos.

"What the hell you want a goddamn line that you can cast eighty feet for?" he asked. "Goddamn trout are only twenty feet away. And you can't turn around one of those weight-forward things when the one end gets worn out. You have to buy a whole new line. That's why they push 'em in stores, you know. You'll come back twice as fast to get a new line 'cause you can only use one end. Bastards."

He occupied the place among curmudgeons that Willie Mays occupies among ballplayers. Perfection. The zenith. A rare natural gift honed by years of practice. A standard to which most men can barely aspire.

I liked him, and he seemed to find me tolerable, perhaps because I, too, fished a cheap fiberglass rod. His profanity was admirable: no scatological words, no crude Anglo-Saxon terms for sexual acts. It consisted mostly of blasphemy, well marbled with references to ille-gitimacy or canine lineage on the maternal side. And for all his cussing and crankiness, Red wasn't angry, except occasionally about having trouble wading the river he'd been fishing since Hoover sat in the White House. His curmudgeonliness was a matter of principle. Some things and people, such as anyone who brought a loud radio near the river, were just goddamn sonofabitching jerky bastards who could go straight to hell, and that was that. It was merely a statement of fact, made, as often as not, with a hint of a smile on his mug.

We talked fishing mostly, sometimes baseball. Red followed the Mets, and indeed wore their cap when fishing, but he'd been a Dodger fan before the goddamn sonsabitches had deserted their fans and gone to California, the greedy bastards. He taught me the real names of the places along the stream, of which I remember only one:

the Mayor's Pool, named after a local politico of the 1930s who loved to fish and usually had to be fetched from the river half an hour after a town meeting had started. I fished the same pool half a century later and was glad to know its name.

Red told me that the river had for many years been in much worse shape, back when the now-defunct factories and mills had discharged all sorts of chemicals and oil into the stream, back before the municipal sewerage system had been built. But even further back, he said, in the early days of the Depression, it had been a lovely stream, clear and almost wild, full of smallmouths. Then the war and industry came, and for a long time Red figured that his river was done for. It was good to see it clear again, he said.

"Goddamn liberals are good for something," he noted. "The lyin' bastards," he added. I had to agree on both counts.

I enjoyed watching him fish for the trout stocked in our little river. He fished the old-fashioned way, roll-casting a wet fly down and across the current and letting it swing, sometimes mending his line, sometimes stripping, sometimes feeding a little slack into the drift. He roll-cast beautifully and smoothly, making his little fiberglass rod bend almost to the butt, throwing the loop of green double-taper line out and across the stream so that the leader popped out of the water and straightened, every time. He didn't have many tricks— I don't think I ever saw him put the line in the air—but those he had were polished to perfection. He caught more trout than I did.

He worked the water slowly, shuffling carefully along a bottom that had grown strangely treacherous over the past decade, the eternal Chesterfield hanging from his lip as he muttered at the fish, calling them sonsabitches and bastards, and yet crooning to them, too. When he had luck, he'd put a brace of small trout in his tattered canvas creel for his wife to cook.

"I just keep some of the little ones," he once told me. "Those big bastards don't taste as good."

One day I watched from the path as Red netted and released a pretty good brown, a plump fourteen-inch fish whose colors hinted that it was a holdover from one of the previous year's stockings. He looked up and saw me as he finished washing his hands in the stream, so he sloshed over to the bank for a smoke and a chat.

"Nice fish," I said, lighting a filtered cigarette that, around Red, always seemed somehow effeminate. He smoked the kind that separated the men from the boys by killing the boys almost immediately.

"Not bad," Red replied. "Son of a bitch sure fought like hell. I won't kill a fish like that."

"What did you get him on?"

"Same thing as always," Red said, handing me his ancient fly rod. A bedraggled wet fly sat in the hookkeeper, a slender, size 12 pattern with a red tail, yellow floss body ribbed with gold, sparse brown hackle, and mallard-flank wing.

"A Professor," I said.

"Good for you," he rasped. "Most of you young guys don't know the old flies. These jerky sonsabitches around here"—he gestured at the world in general, taking in, I supposed, all of our fellow anglers—"wouldn't know a goddamn Professor if you stuck it in their ass. That's all I use, these days. Got a whole box of 'em."

He wasn't kidding. His one fly box, a slender aluminum thing with little spring-steel clips inside, held Professors in half a dozen sizes tied on several styles of hooks. Besides a bunch made on traditional Sproat wet-fly hooks, he had some on nymph hooks and a few on small, long-shank streamer irons. That was it: Professors and more Professors.

"That's it?" I asked. "Just Professors?" I hadn't expected to learn that Red toted a portable entomology lab in his stained, ripped, Chesterfield-burned vest—his decrepit tackle, cheap when it was new, indicated an immunity to trendiness—but I had him pegged as a guy who had learned some of the buggy secrets of our little river.

"Sure, that's it. What the hell else do I need? See, when the water's low like this, I fish one of them little ones. Roll 'er out there and let 'er swing. When the water's high and dirty, I use a bigger one with a little split shot on the leader. Fish it real slow, right along the bottom."

"And that always works? One Professor or another?"

"Hell, no. Nothin' *always* works. What the hell do you want something that always works for? Sometimes the bastards don't want anything. Sometimes the water's too goddamn high and only a jack-ass goes fishing." He was warming to his subject. "So what? Think you're gonna catch every fish in the stream just because you carry ten pounds of flies? You'll learn. If they don't want a little yellow fly or a big yellow fly or a medium goddamn yellow fly, then the sons-abitches can go straight to hell for all I care. I've caught enough of them in my life, and if they don't want none of these flies I figure it out pretty quick. I go home and watch the ball game on the TV. Though sometimes I wonder why I bother. You see that game last night? Goddamn sonsabitches played like a bunch of pansies." And he began a description of the bottom of the eighth, in which a fatal error by the New York shortstop set up two unearned runs that cost the Mets the game. His profanity, particularly that referring to divine condemnation of canine lineage on the maternal side, reached new heights. He loved baseball almost as much as fishing.

I saw Red a few more times before I got married and moved to another town. I'd watch him shuffling along on spindly octogenarian legs as he roll-cast one of his Professors across the stream, the thirti-eth unfiltered cigarette of the day dangling from his bottom lip, his droopy old yellow fly rod following the drift of a cheap, cracked, double-taper green line, crooning profanity at the trout as he fished a stream he'd known since the days when he drove a Model A.

And it occurred to me, years after the last summer that Red and I shared the river, that I'd met a man who'd attained a certain state of grace, a guy who'd figured out what mattered to him and whose world made perfect sense. I hope he's now in a place where, every now and then, one of the really big bastards tilts up off the bottom of the Mayor's Pool and sucks in a size 12 Professor and then fights like two sonsabitches.

The canal had once crossed the state and linked the Delaware River with the ocean. It was built when there were still living veterans of the Revolution, and it had been one of the engineering marvels and commercial arteries of a young nation. But railroads and then trucks moved goods more efficiently, and the canal went out of business during Woodrow Wilson's second term. Most of it was filled in by fools and developers after it shut down, but a few stretches survived.

I lived near a section of the canal for eight years. A diversion from a little river fed the upstream end of this segment, and the water ran out of the downstream end three-quarters of a mile away and returned to the river. The flow kept the canal supplied with cool, well-aerated water and gave it a barely perceptible current. Lush weed beds covered about half of the bottom, and the water was as clear as a bonefish flat.

Back when it was whole, the canal had drawn most of its water from the state's largest natural lake. It had run near and drawn more water from several small rivers. The western end exchanged water with the Delaware River. Over time, the canal had acquired nearly every type of freshwater fish that lived in the state, and my section still held most of them. Largemouth bass, smallmouths, pickerel, yellow perch, bullheads, crappies, bluegills, rock bass, pumpkinseeds, redear sunfish, carp, suckers, creek chubs, and shiners all lived in the canal. The bass, for some reason, rarely got big, but the perch, crappies, and pickerel grew to above-average sizes.

A wall of trees along the old towpath made the canal a tough place for fly casting, and the fish usually spurned plugs, spinners, and other lures. I think the water was too clear and the habitat too rich for artificial baits to work. Any fly or lure that I cast into the canal looked as obviously phony as a candidate on the stump a month before election day.

But the canal was a marvelous place to fish a live shiner under a float. If you sat perfectly still in the tall grass, you would eventually notice that a bass or pickerel had materialized six feet away from the minnow. You never saw the fish coming; suddenly it was just there, hovering in the water and eyeballing the bait. Then you'd hold your breath and send telepathic messages to persuade the fish to eat. The unfortunate shiner, its day already ruined by the size 2 hook through its back, would get wind of the predator and start to swim away, dragging the red and white float across the canal. The bass or pickerel would follow, seeming to glide without moving a fin, maintaining its distance as it made up its mind. And you'd sit there in the tall grass, not moving a muscle except to open the bail on the reel so that the fish could run with the bait, watching the bass or pickerel and thinking *eat it, eat it, eat it.*

The attack was always exciting and usually instructive. Bass and pickerel kill shiners in different ways. A bass would often suck in the minnow and chomp on it and blow it out several times before truly eating it. My wife theorized that the fish was tenderizing its lunch, and that's a pretty accurate assessment. I have watched a bass in an aquarium suck in a crayfish, chew on the crustacean for a few seconds (if "chew" is the right word for what a bass does in its throat), and then blow out the claws before swallowing the crushed body. The same bass would inhale a live goldfish, scale the minnow in its throat, and then exhale a cloud of tiny scales. Bass often eat very deliberately, and watching one take a shiner in the canal was like watching a cat play with a rodent.

A pickerel's attack was always too fast for the eye to follow. One instant the fish was four feet away from the bait, and then you blinked and the pickerel had the shiner in its cruel mouth and was already moving away. Then came the delicious suspense of letting the fish run with the bait. You had to wait until the pickerel stopped, released the dead shiner so that it could swallow the minnow head first, and started moving off again with the entire bait inside its mouth. Only then could you strike and hook the fish and finally exhale.

I have watched tarpon and bonefish change direction to take a fly. I've seen a trout with a head as wide as my fist poke its snout into the air to take a big Irresistible bouncing down a deep, fast run. And I've seen the bow wave thrown up by a redfish charging a crab pattern in murky water. Those are grand sights and I'm lucky to have enjoyed them. But none of them was as intensely interesting as watching a shiner meet its fate in the canal. I've had no finer fishing than those days on a remnant of a defunct commercial waterway.

Mary Jo and I went to the canal often when we were dating and first married. For the price of two dozen shiners we could get away from the world for an afternoon. It was leisurely, no-pressure fishing, perfect sport for a couple. We'd sit in the tall grass and talk and watch our floats, content to leave the decisions to the fish.

We went there with a bucket of bait on a cool, sunny late-October day the year before we were married. We soaked shiners for about an hour without a bite, then Mary Jo lay back on the bank and closed her eyes.

"Wake me up if you see my float go under," she said. I promised that I would and moved down the canal to try another spot. Mary Jo dozed in the sunshine, her hat over her eyes and her rod lying across her stomach.

She was awakened by the rod sliding off her body. I looked up when she yelled and saw her hanging on to the rod with both hands. It was my heavy spinning outfit with which I'd caught redfish in Florida, and it was bent to the butt. I started to crank in my bait, then something very big made a yard-wide swirl on the surface, and I set my rod down in the grass and started running up the towpath. As I got close to Mary Jo, I heard the buzz of the drag as her fish took more of the 10-pound line from the spool.

*It must be a hell of a big bass,* I thought.

Mary Jo held on until the fish turned, and then began slowly to recover line. Whenever the fish lunged, she had to let go of the reel and resume her two-handed grip on the rod.

"What do you think it is? Jesus, it's strong."

"Probably a big bass," I said. "Just keep steady pressure on him. No sudden jerks. Let him wear himself out."

"I think he's gonna wear me out. Christ, he's strong."

Then we saw that it wasn't a bass but an immense pickerel, the biggest one I'd ever seen. As Mary Jo pumped the long, green fish a little closer, I began to think that maybe it was the biggest pickerel *anyone* had ever seen. Had it been a northern pike, it would have been a respectable specimen.

Naturally, we did not have a net. And the fish was much too big to grab with my hands.

I found a spot where the grass grew down to the very edge of the water. "See if you can steer him here," I said.

Pickerel aren't blessed in the stamina department, and Mary Jo was able to guide the fish toward me. *Jesus, he's immense,* I thought. I saw that the fish had hooked itself in the corner of the mouth when it had run with the bait, and that neither the hard-mono snell nor the line had suffered any abrasion from the pickerel's teeth.

"Just guide him toward me," I said, "and I'll try to slide him up on the bank."

I had my hand on the line when the fish made one last surge toward the middle of the canal.

"Oh shit oh shit oh shit," Mary Jo said. "*Please* don't get off."

"It's okay. Just lead him back here again."

Then my right foot was in the water and I had my hand on the line and felt the knot where it joined the snell. I lifted just enough to raise the massive head out of the water, and then slid the great fish up onto the grass. It flopped twice and lay still, its huge gill covers opening and closing. Mary Jo and I knelt on either side of it. I pushed on the hook and it slipped out of the fish's jaw.

I sat on the grass so that I could measure the fish against my leg. When my heel was even with the pickerel's tail, the fish could have turned its head and bitten me in the ass. The nose reached to the back pocket of my jeans. That's more than three feet from my heel. Then I measured it against the spinning rod and scratched a tiny mark on the blank. Later, a tape measure established that the scratch was a bit more than thirty-seven inches above the bottom of the rod.

We had a decision to make, and fast.

"I think this is a world-record fish," I said. "Hell, I *know* it's a record. What do you want to do?"

"This fish is really old, isn't it?" Mary Jo asked.

"Yep."

"It's like a dinosaur or something," she said. "Look at its eyes. This fish isn't afraid of anything. Put it back."

"You sure?"

"Yes. I don't want it to die."

I wet my hands at the edge of the canal and lifted the fish and slid it back into the water. It lay on its side, not moving except for its gills. Pickerel often go into shock when they're caught. Sometimes they recover, but sometimes they don't.

I gave the fish a push and it drifted away from the bank, still on its side, still motionless except for the feeble movement of its gill covers.

"Don't die, fish," Mary Jo said. "I'm sorry. Don't die."

And then without another word she was in the canal. The water couldn't have been much over 50 degrees, and she gasped when it reached her thighs. She leaned over and cradled the pickerel, holding it upright and moving it slowly to force water over its gills.

"C'mon, fish," she said. "Wake up. Don't die. Jesus, it's cold."

After what seemed like a long time but couldn't have been more than thirty seconds, the fish came to. It swam away slowly at first, then darted into a patch of weeds. We saw the weeds moving as the pickerel swam through them, and then it was gone.

I helped Mary Jo out of the water. She stood on the bank, soaked to the hips and shivering. I dumped the rest of the bait into the canal and started collecting our tackle.

"How old do you think that fish was?" Mary Jo asked.

"I don't know. Old. Ten years, maybe more. They live a long time. That might be the oldest pickerel in the world."

"I hope he's okay. Or is it a she? Isn't it probably a girl?"

"Probably," I said. "Almost certainly a girl. The males don't get nearly that big." We had walked down to where I'd dropped my rod. I picked it up and we were ready to go. Mary Jo was still shivering.

"'Bye, fish," she said to the canal. "Thank you. You sure were fun. I hope you have lots of babies next year."

Only a fool would not marry a girl who does things like that.

*South Carolina, 2002*

## CHAPTER 16

# *Pens for Hire*

THERE'S A SHORT PAUSE IN THE FRENZY OF MAGAZINE MAKING after an issue has been consigned to the pre-press house. During this lull, which might last as long as half a day, I tunnel into the mountain of mail on my desk and grope for journalistic nuggets. Most of the time, I must be content to extract a tiny pile of ore that can be refined into workable metal and a larger pile of worthless tailings.

Some of the mail, however, is twenty-four karat.

> *Reg Southerby*
> *P.O. Box 666*
> *Elk Wallow, Wyoming*

*Mr. Art Scheck*
*Fly Flinger Magazine*
*Maplebury, Vermont*

*Good Morning, Art,*

I'm suspicious of any letter that begins with the sort of bogus bonhomie you hear from real-estate peddlers. But I read on; even a carnival barker might know something about angling.

*Casa Braggadocio Lodge, located on the white-sand beaches of a private island off the west coast of Java, is world renowned for large catches of world-class billfish, many topping the 150-lb. mark. For the fly angler seeking the ultimate in bluewater thrills, Casa Braggadocio is a trip to fly-fishing heaven. On a recent visit, myself and two companions boated 438 sailfish and marlin in six days, all taken on flies. Seventeen of the fish would have broken existing world records but were released for conservation reasons.*

Yep, it has the earmarks of the work of a sporting shill: scads of clichés—at least a half dozen in the first two sentences—and a couple of doubtful claims that can't be checked. Although I have a pretty fair idea of what's coming, I persevere.

*I'm sure you'll agree that Fly Flinger's readers would like to hear about the opportunities for once-in-a-lifetime action at Casa Braggadocio. In fact, I'm so sure you'll agree that I've taken the liberty of sending the enclosed 2,500-word feature article, along with 30 color slides. I realize that this approach is a little out of the ordinary, and I'm sure you usually prefer to work from queries, but this is a story that just can't wait. Naturally, I'll be glad to go along with any editorial changes or suggestions you have in mind— the important thing, Art, is to get the story of this truly incredible fishing in front of your readers. Please take a look at the article and get back to me as soon as you can. I'm offering this story to several magazines, because I feel so strongly about its value to serious fly fishers.*

*Also enclosed is a copy of a letter from Greg Packemin, owner of Casa Braggadocio, which I'm sure you'll find interesting.*

*Looking forward to your reply,*
*Reg Southerby*

This boy missed his calling, I think. He could have cleaned up selling junk bonds.

I can guess the general drift of the epistle from Mr. Packemin without reading it, but I scan it just to check my instincts. Beneath the Casa Braggadocio coat of arms—a marlin rampant on a field of ballyhoo—is the slogan "Ultimate Adventure for the Serious Angler," followed by his message.

> *Dear Editor,*
>
> *Casa Braggadocio, the world's foremost destination for offshore fly fishermen, is eager to expand its advertising in select publications such as yours. Should you decide to publish Mr. Southerby's article, we are prepared to sign a contract guaranteeing the purchase of three four-color full-page advertisements. Please have your advertising representative send me your rate card and mechanical specifications at your earliest convenience.*
>
> > *Sincerely,*
> > *Greg Packemin*

Mr. Packemin's letter contains no superfluous embroidery: if I print a promotional piece about his operation, he'll spend money with the company that issues my paycheck. Even a rustic editor unschooled in the workings of business can understand such an approach. I'd have more time to fish if more writers had such an exemplary grasp of concision.

My usual procedure for dealing with this sort of dreck is to stuff the manuscript, unread, into a return envelope, along with the slides and a brief note informing the writer that I'm absolutely swamped with articles and can't possibly accept a thing until sometime around the Apocalypse. Then I pass along a copy of the letter from the lodge owner to our advertising director, on the off chance that we might be able to drum up some legitimate business. Finally, the cover letters go into a file labeled "Whores and Pimps," which I maintain for my own amusement.

But this time, since I have a few minutes to waste, I take a quick gander at the manuscript. The lead, a predictable yarn about a jumping fish, a screaming reel, and a triumphant angler, contains no surprises. Midway through the second page, however, as the author fills in the background of his story, I'm arrested by a sentence: "The tales of incredible catches being made routinely at Casa Braggadocio were almost too much to believe, and it was only natural for *Fly Flinger* to send me there to check the truth of the stories for its readers."

Clearly, the old bean is not what it was. I can't imagine how I forgot having made such an unusual assignment. Yet I must have forgotten. The alternative—that I'm being played for a chump by a couple of hucksters—is unthinkable. These chaps wouldn't just *assume* that the contents of a magazine are for sale, would they?

Indeed they might, and sometimes they're right. When I was still damp behind the editorial ears, I took umbrage at such shenanigans. Not anymore, though; you get used to anything after a while. And so Reg gets a bland letter of refusal, and the file devoted to hustlers becomes a little thicker.

Not every pitch is in writing. Some outfits prefer telemarketing. The phone rings before I can dig any deeper into my mountain of mail.

"*Hey*, Art, how ya doin'?" In five words, the caller lets me know that he's mastered the art of acting sincere. I wish he'd let me know his name. I say I'm fine but just a mite busy, hoping to discourage a harangue. I can smell a drummer even over the phone.

"Hey, I know how it is, and I won't take up much of your time. That's a helluva good magazine you folks put out. I was reading it just this morning, and I thought I'd give you a call before it got too late in the day. My name's Jeff Handler, and I've been doing some work with Circle Barcode Ranch out here in Idaho. Are you familiar with the Circle Barcode, Art?"

I confess my ignorance; just don't get around much anymore.

"Well, hey, maybe I'm a little prejudiced, but I don't think there's another place like it on earth. Forty-five-hundred acres, seventeen miles of private water, two of the prettiest spring creeks you can imagine, four chefs straight from Paris, the best guides in the West, and a five-star lodge with hot tubs, waterbeds, and honeymoon suites with mirrored ceilings."

I summon my command of the western idiom and admit that it sounds like a mighty fine spread.

"It is, Art. You've never seen anything like it. But hey, I bet the fishing is what would excite you the most. We were out on the river yesterday morning and caught fifty-three rainbows, none less than twenty-two inches. And all on dry flies—we had a PMD hatch you wouldn't believe. It was a blizzard—an absolute blizzard. We finally quit because we were too tired to cast, but the fish were still rising."

I make noises to indicate that I'm impressed.

"I knew you'd be impressed. And that was just an average day— you should see it when the salmonflies come off! Anyway, Art, what I was wondering is this: How'd you like to come out to the Circle Barcode for a week as our guest and catch a few fish? The PMDs should keep coming off for a few weeks yet, then we've got hoppers and a fall *Baetis* hatch that'll blow your mind. It'd make a great piece for your magazine, and I bet your readers would love to know about a place like this."

Ah, yes, the other approach. Instead of working the advertising angle (which can be risky; some editors are not noted for business acumen), sometimes it's better to make a personal offer, to propose a little swap between friends: hospitality and fish in exchange for coverage in the gazette.

Why not? I need a vacation. I'd sure like to catch a few dozen huge trout every day for a week. And some of the readers probably would enjoy a story about the Circle Barcode Ranch. Most of them will never see such a place, and very few can afford such angling, but so what? An occasional junket to a swank lodge is one of the perks of an editor's job, right? And a fellow can't just accept first-class hospitality for *nothing,* can he? Naturally, I'll be obligated to write a story in which every cast brings a strike from a two-foot-long wild trout and the skies are not cloudy all day. But, hell, it's just a *fish story.* It's not like a fly-fishing rag is supposed to be hard news.

It's a seductive line of reasoning. Like many rationalizations, it's bolstered by the knowledge that if I don't do it, somebody else will.

Somebody else will have to. I have rules and a hellish schedule that promises to keep me indoors for the rest of the season. I tell Jeff that I can't accept his offer.

"Hey, that's too bad, Art. But maybe you can send a writer out. Reg Southerby, for instance. He's pretty good at destination coverage. I've got his number around here someplace. If you want, I'll call him and set the whole thing up."

Sure, that would make it all right. There's nothing wrong with commissioning a freelancer to compose a dithyramb in trade for a free trip. Hey, maybe the Circle Barcode will even buy an ad, to run next to the last page of the article.

I try to be polite in these circumstances. Jeff is just doing his job. I tell him I'm terribly sorry, but I'm awash in articles and can't possibly assign anything to anyone right now.

"Hey, Art, I'm sorry to hear that. Maybe next year."

I hope Jeff doesn't think I'm rude if he can't reach me on his first try next year and I can't find time to return his call. I'm a pretty busy guy, and there's no telling what I might be doing when he calls.

I might be occupied by the overtures of another lodge. The Circle Barcode isn't the only joint with mirrored hot tubs full of expensive whiskey and six-pound trout. Nor is it the only destination with a press-relations man who'd like me to sign on as his junior partner.

Or I might be tied up fending off the advances of a manufacturer who'd like me to review a product he's sure will brighten the lives of my readers, a product the tackle maker would be happy to let me keep when I'm done with my glowing writeup. The sporting-goods business is among the last redoubts of generosity in a stingy world, though a colleague during my own brief stint as a publicity flack put it more crassly: "When we find a writer who's good to us, it pays to keep him greased."

Or perhaps, when Mr. Handler calls again, I'll be deep within another mountain of mail, looking for nuggets or perusing a manuscript that strikes me as a tad suspect, objectivitywise. Some of my mail is worth dawdling over, especially the pieces that leave me agog at the complexity of schemes in which it's hard to tell who's greasing whom.

Something like the next submission in the pile, for instance, an unsolicited piece from Sid Greesepalm, a chap often described in biographical notes as "a veteran outdoor writer."

> *Our float plane banked hard to the left and began its descent through the clouds above Big Mooserump Lake. As we came out of the turn, I caught my first glimpse of the immaculate white cabins of Big Mooserump Lodge (P.O. Box 64, Hoarfrost, Ontario, Canada), a world-class angling resort where, ten minutes later, we were greeted by our genial hosts, Abner and Sarie Mae Winthrop. After one of Sarie Mae's incomparable home-cooked lunches, Abner explained that we'd arrived at an opportune time.*
>
> *"Fishing's been even better than usual," he noted as he sipped his liebfraumilch, one of the many vintages in the lodge's unsurpassed cellar. "One fellow who was here last week boated ninety-six pike over four feet, and every one of them took a popper. They should still be easy to take on top. And the lakers are still in the shallows—I missed a shot at a thirty-pounder on a dry fly the other day."*

The next few paragraphs follow the formula. Fairly atremble with anticipation, the author and his chums rig up and head for the dock, where they are met by their guide, Zack Stereotype, an Ojibway right out of Central Casting, who runs them to the nearest hot spot in a craft as comfortable as it is seaworthy. The author makes note of the breathtaking scenery as the (insert brand name here) boat flashes across the mirrorlike lake. They round a rocky point, enter a cove, and shut down the (insert brand name here) outboard. Their first casts, predictably, are greeted with success.

> *The Delrin-and-titanium drag of my Whalestopper IV reel howled in protest as a fifty-four-inch northern streaked across the shallow bay. Shaking its enormous head in fury, the pike turned and bulled its way toward a tangle of limbs where two pine trees had toppled into the lake.*
>
> *"You'd better stop him quick," Zack muttered. "If he gets into that blowdown, you'll lose him for sure."*
>
> *I reared back on the experimental 8-weight Rocket-Rod that the Goniff & Gardyloo Company had asked me to test on the behemoths of the North. New, untried gear makes me nervous, and though the Rocket-Rod had already proved an unsurpassed casting instrument, I couldn't help wondering how much strain such a featherweight stick could take.*
>
> *Plenty, as it turned out. The Rocket-Rod's plaited-boron butt easily turned the giant pike away from the submerged branches and into open water, where the Whalestopper's space-age drag quickly wore the fish down. Minutes later, I released my first Big Mooserump pike, one of many my friends and I were to catch in the coming days.*
>
> *Abner's prediction of topwater action turned out to be right on the money. Indeed, of the 214 pike we boated, nearly every one fell for a chartreuse size 2/0 Burbleblaster, a unique foam-bodied popper/slider/diver I've developed specifically for trophy pike. Our six largest fish, however, took my weedless Perchy-Poos fished deep with the new Bathylinear Mark II super-fast-sinking lines.*

It pains me to send back such a classic of the genre. That the trip to Big Mooserump was a freebie I can safely assume, having declined the junket myself. That the author is a paid "consultant" for Whalestopper Reels is common knowledge in the industry, though perhaps not among readers. That he was given a couple of Rocket Rods in exchange for ink is more than likely; I, too, have been offered the honor of eulogizing the new wondersticks. Ditto the Bathylinear fly lines. The author's infallible pike flies, he neglects to mention, are made and marketed by a company that pays him a royalty.

It's as close to a perfect piece as any I've seen, lacking only endorsements of the float plane and the liebfraumilch. Such unity of theme is much to be admired; not everyone can make plugola work as a leitmotif.

But back it must go. I have a quirky reluctance to inflict such bilge on unsuspecting readers, and by the time I overhauled the piece to excise its excesses, I'd be lucky to have a caption left. It's tempting to make a photocopy, just to have a model in case I ever have to fall back on writing formulaic puffery to make a living. But to steal another man's tools would be irredeemably wrong, a violation of my profession's code of ethics.

Besides, when I need someday to hire out my pen to keep the wolves away, I think I'll try something different, maybe look for a literary field less slimy than the outdoor-ink game.

Pornographic novels, for instance.

*Vermont, 1996*

## CHAPTER 17

# *Evenings in June*

FOR A FEW WEEKS EARLY IN THE SUMMER, THE ARBOGAST JITTER-bug stands unrivaled among the works of man. Not that other top-water lures won't catch bass. Lots of them do. The Hula Popper has its moments, as does the Zara Puppy and the Tiny Torpedo and that most unlikely of surface lures, a lead-head buzzbait with a chattering aluminum blade. And when you have to work the shallow, weedy water a foot from the bank, a deer-hair fly-rod bug sometimes out-fishes any specimen of hardware.

But a Jitterbug is my favorite bait during the magic weeks. Sen-timent, I suppose. Dad and I fished with Jitterbugs when I was a boy. When I was grown and he had a boat on Greenwood Lake, we'd go out at dusk and fish until after midnight, throwing big black Jitter-bugs as far into the darkness as we could and cranking them back, maybe with the boat's radio turned up just enough for us to hear the Mets game. We'd listen to the play-by-play by Ralph Kiner or Lind-say Nelson and to the soft *plip-plip-plip-plip* of our lures walking across the water, and then forget the game when we'd hear the sud-den *shloop* of a bass taking one of them and the splashes as the fish tried to throw the plug. It was good fishing, full of mystery, with every little sound magnified by the night.

Sentiment aside, I get a kick out of these old-fashioned lures. They've been around since FDR was president, back when plug rods were made of steel and a guy needed a hefty forearm to use one and a well-educated thumb to control a South Bend Perfectoreno reel filled with braided line.

I'm partial to jointed, three-eighths-ounce Jitterbugs with a froggy paint job. I modify them, reinforcing the screw-in hardware with epoxy and reorienting the hook hangers so I can add split rings and replace the treble hooks with barbless doubles. I like how they cast, I love the sound they make on the water, and I'll never tire of the way largemouths hit them. Nothing else is like a Jitterbug strike. A bass might make more noise and a bigger splash blowing up on a popper or a Zara Puppy, but it grabs a Jitterbug with a sudden violence that takes my breath away even after seeing and hearing it hundreds of times. I've often wondered if a fish really wanted to eat the thing or just kill it out of meanness; I swear that sometimes I've heard the plug's hardware rattle in that split second when a bass pounces.

And I suppose I enjoy throwing a Jitterbug because it's not an all-season-long, all-conditions lure. Where I fish, it works best during a short spell somewhere between Memorial Day and the Fourth of July, and then only in the evenings. It belongs to my favorite times and places, and to the fish I like better than any other.

On a good evening in June, I can hear the frogs booming and croaking the instant I shut down the car in the parking lot a hundred yards from the pond in the middle of town. I listen to the symphony of three species of amphibians calling for mates as I tighten a Lew's Speed Spool or Ambassadeur reel in the seat of a plug rod, string the 10-pound-test line through the guides, tie on a jointed Jitterbug with a loop knot, adjust the reel's drag and cast control, and drench myself with bug repellent. There's no hurry as I assemble my tackle. The last

hour before the bats come out—sometimes only the last half hour—
is all that interests me. A pair of needle-nose pliers goes in a back
pocket, in case a big fish takes the plug deep. I bring nothing else; I
will catch bass the way I like best, or I won't catch them.

I walk through the gap in the rickety split-rail fence and follow
the path through the tall grass toward the far end of the pond, keeping away from the water and treading softly, watching for swirls in
the shallows and trying to guess which are made by bedding bluegills
and which reveal largemouths on the hunt. If it's one of the warm
and muggy evenings of which we have too few in New England, the
humid air carries the scents of water and weeds and spawning
bluegills to my nose.

By the time I've reached the end of the path, I've shut out the
sounds of cars a hundred yards away on Main Street. For the next
hour, the world will shrink to this little piece of water.

It's hard to imagine a better place to be a largemouth bass or a
fisherman. The pond is roughly square, perhaps three hundred yards
on each side. It has an island that, in a few places, I can just reach
with a long cast. Two sides of the pond are open country, one has a
few breaks in the trees from which I can cast, and the fourth side is
a jungle a monkey couldn't penetrate. That side, I know, holds some
big fish I could get to with a float tube or canoe. I've seen the tall
wakes and huge splashes of bass killing baby bluegills and frogs in the
shallow water along the overgrown bank. But I decided long ago not
to fish that part of the pond. The bass deserve a sanctuary, a nursery
for the yearlings and a rest home for the big old gals that have
spawned many broods.

If the pond had a few big trees sunk in the deep water, it could
teach a guy nearly everything he needs to know about bass fishing.
Even without drowned timber, it's the most complete school and
laboratory I've ever found.

A spring enters through a culvert on the side nearest Main Street.
Close to the northwest corner, behind thick stands of cattails, smaller

springs trickle into the pond and keep the ground muddy even during a drought. Later in the season, during the hottest weather, bass gather in the cool water coming in from the spring and the little seeps.

On a warm evening in June, though, they could be anywhere along the banks, chasing small fish or waiting for a frog to make its last mistake. They like frogs, my bass do. "Calcium," a friend theorizes. Frogs have hard skeletons full of calcium that bass need but don't get enough of from dragonfly nymphs and baby sunfish. The pond lacks crayfish, leaving frogs as the best bone-building supplement in the largemouths' diet. Sounds reasonable to me.

A dozen times over the years, I've watched fishing-magazine clichés come to life when a big bass made the water bulge and boil a second after a bullfrog or leopard frog hopped into the pond. You almost expect to see a blood slick. Once, not a hundred feet from me, one of the big sows pinned a frog right against the bank, throwing muddy water into the air and making a sound like a pig rooting in its slop.

Several years ago, my wife and I spotted a tremendous commotion against the shore of the island, right where a frog had been singing.

"See that?" I asked. "Nature red in tooth and claw."

"Cool," Mary Jo said. "Poor froggie jumped in the wrong spot. Catch that fish." She has an exaggerated confidence in my abilities.

Still, it wasn't an opportunity to pass up. I threw a two-handed cast at the island and got lucky: the reel didn't overrun, and the Jitterbug splashed down within a yard of the target. I had cranked it perhaps two feet when a bulge and then a wake formed behind the plug, and then the bass crashed the lure and sent it flipping through the air in a spray of water.

*"Beautiful,"* I said. "Perfect. God *damn,* that was good." It didn't matter that I had missed the fish. For a second or two, this had been the best of all possible worlds. And I had been running it.

That's why I love June evenings. The best of them are perfect in ways that almost nothing else approaches.

It's not that I always knock 'em dead, though every now and then I do. One astonishing evening, I landed twenty-one bass and missed another half a dozen in little more than an hour. A couple times, I've caught a dozen or so. Most nights in June, though, I'm glad to hook three or four, and I've been skunked more than once.

And it's not as though I expect to set the new state record. My best-ever bass from the pond might have weighed five pounds. Over eight years, I've caught maybe six that weighed on the better side of three pounds, and ten or twelve that I'd reckon were two-pound fish. A local kid claims to have caught a seven-pounder, and I like to believe that he did. But most of my June fish are garden-variety small-pond largemouths, males an inch on either side of a foot long. They're snotty, strong, high-jumping fish with a grandiose view of their own appetites, but tackle busters they ain't.

It doesn't matter. It's enough to know that the pond holds a few bruisers, and to believe that once every so many casts my plug will land in front of one that's disposed to eat it. Mostly, it's enough to fish well, to make accurate casts and feel the spool turning beneath my thumb, to hear the solid mechanical *chunk* when the reel's gears engage, to steer the goofy old-fashioned lure around the early lily pads, to shift the rod to my right hand at the end of a retrieve and click the reel into freespool and do it all again. As the light starts to fade and the frogs get louder, the springtime seeps through my skin and the long winter is finally banished.

As I throw and crank, throw and crank, listening to the frogs and feeling dew soak through my sneakers, the boundary between me and the June evening softens and becomes permeable. Stillwater mayflies and caddisflies, some emerging and others laying eggs, ride the surface of the pond. The sunfish eat the insects and the frogs eat the insects, and the bass eat the frogs and sunfish. A heron stalks the edge of the island, hoping to spear a frog or a small fish. Birds skim the water, snatching bugs out of the air. One of the big turtles, throwback to the age of dinosaurs, pokes its head up to take a breath. A baby muskrat swims by, then takes fright at my movements and vanishes beneath the surface. Bluegills and pumpkinseeds scurry back and forth in the shallows, looking for mates and chasing rivals. The water heaves against the bank fifty yards away as a bass finds a frog. A bullfrog on the edge of the island, a fat old king among frogs, croaks his courtship song, the ballooning yellow sac of his throat visible even in the gloaming.

It's alive. Everything around me is fiercely, intensely *alive,* eating and trying to avoid being eaten, making a nest or breeding or guarding eggs, constantly on the move, whether driven by hunger, fear, or lust. Out in the pond, my Jitterbug, a lure thrown by my homemade rod and connected by sixty feet of monofilament to the reel cupped in my left hand, waddles across the water, going *plip-plip-plip-plip* as I make it swim, looking like prey or maybe something that simply needs killing. And maybe a bass comes up to eat it, mistaking the plastic and metal lure for a frog. Then the rod bucks in my hand, the bass jumps, and I laugh like a boy, not caring if the fish throws the plug. Tonight, I fish for the strike and that wonderful first jump, for the moment when a man with an office job and bills and worries, a guy who came perilously close to losing the perfect, ineffable, marrow-deep magic of the strike and the jump, connects with the life in the pond.

Then I make another cast and enjoy it as much as the last one. I will keep casting into the June evening until I can barely see the lure coming across the water, until the bats come swarming out of their hidey-holes and my childish fear of them drives me from the pond. For a while, though, I feel that if the hour could last forever, I could stand here and throw good casts and catch good bass until the end of time, and then go to my Judgment reeking of bug dope and fish slime and with a big grin on my mug.

In a good year with what passes for normal weather in New England, the best evening fishing doesn't last long. If we're lucky, we get a month of it. Twenty-eight days, say. Knock off half a dozen days for bad weather and that many more for responsibilities, and we have sixteen left—in a good year.

Then remember that we're talking about hours in the evening, not full days. Let's be optimistic and say that I can squeeze 90 minutes of at least hopeful fishing out of each of my sixteen evenings. That makes 1,440 minutes, or 24 hours.

One day of wonder and hope and perfection out of a year. It hardly seems enough, hardly seems fair. Yet it's more than some anglers get, as they'd learn if they did the math.

But it's enough, because that day, those hours and minutes, stick in the memory and let you remember what's real and who you are. Evenings in June get you through the winter, through the foolishness and frustrations of work, through the bad times when a fat bass jumping out of a clear pond seems a million miles and a thousand years away.

They get you through.

*Vermont, 2001*